On Political Impasse

ALSO AVAILABLE FROM BLOOMSBURY

The Primacy of Resistance: Power, Opposition and Becoming,
Marco Checchi
Force and Understanding: Writings on Philosophy and Resistance,
Howard Caygill, ed. Stephen Howard
The Ethics of Resistance: Tyranny of the Absolute, Drew M. Dalton
Resistance, Revolution and Fascism: Zapatismo and Assemblage Politics,
Anthony Faramelli
Hegel and Resistance: History, Politics and Dialectics, ed. Bart Zantvoort
and Rebecca Comay
On Resistance: A Philosophy of Defiance, Howard Caygill

On Political Impasse

Power, Resistance, and New Forms of Selfhood

ANTONIO CALCAGNO

BLOOMSBURY ACADEMIC
LONDON • NEW YORK • OXFORD • NEW DELHI • SYDNEY

BLOOMSBURY ACADEMIC
Bloomsbury Publishing Plc
50 Bedford Square, London, WC1B 3DP, UK
1385 Broadway, New York, NY 10018, USA
29 Earlsfort Terrace, Dublin 2, Ireland

BLOOMSBURY, BLOOMSBURY ACADEMIC and the Diana logo
are trademarks of Bloomsbury Publishing Plc

First published in Great Britain 2022

Copyright © Antonio Calcagno, 2022

Antonio Calcagno has asserted his right under the Copyright, Designs
and Patents Act, 1988, to be identified as Author of this work.

For legal purposes the Acknowledgments on p. xi constitute
an extension of this copyright page.

Cover design: *La Pensée*, Auguste Rodin (1901) (conceived 1895)
Cover image © The Picture Art Collection / Alamy Stock Photo

All rights reserved. No part of this publication may be reproduced or transmitted
in any form or by any means, electronic or mechanical, including photocopying,
recording, or any information storage or retrieval system, without prior
permission in writing from the publishers.

Bloomsbury Publishing Plc does not have any control over, or responsibility for,
any third-party websites referred to or in this book. All internet addresses given
in this book were correct at the time of going to press. The author and publisher
regret any inconvenience caused if addresses have changed or sites have ceased
to exist, but can accept no responsibility for any such changes.

A catalogue record for this book is available from the British Library.

Library of Congress Cataloging-in-Publication Data
Names: Calcagno, Antonio, 1969- author.
Title: On political impasse : power, resistance, and
new forms of selfhood / Antonio Calcagno.
Description: London ; New York : Bloomsbury Academic, 2022. |
Includes bibliographical references and index.
Identifiers: LCCN 2021030310 (print) | LCCN 2021030311 (ebook) |
ISBN 9781350268470 (hardback) | ISBN 9781350268487 (pdf) |
ISBN 9781350268494 (ebook)
Subjects: LCSH: Power (Social sciences)–Philosophy. |
Resistance (Philosophy) | Self (Philosophy)
Classification: LCC JC330 .C28 2022 (print) | LCC JC330 (ebook) | DDC 320.01/1–dc23
LC record available at https://lccn.loc.gov/2021030310
LC ebook record available at https://lccn.loc.gov/2021030311

ISBN:	HB:	978-1-3502-6847-0
	ePDF:	978-1-3502-6848-7
	eBook:	978-1-3502-6849-4

Typeset by Integra Software Services Pvt. Ltd.

To find out more about our authors and books visit www.bloomsbury.com
and sign up for our newsletters.

"Ares, arei, sumbalei, dika, dika…"
"Violence upon violence calling forth justice and more justice…"
—Aeschylus, *The Libation-Bearers*

For Fadi Abou-Rihan
—sempre

CONTENTS

Acknowledgments xi
Thesis xii
Preface xiii

1 The New Impasse 1
    Deeper Conditions of the Contemporary Impasse: The Fatigue of Forms of Change and the Rise of a New Form of Political Impasse 1

2 The Inscription of the Ruler–Ruled Power Relation in Political Thought and the Obscuring of Impasse 19
    Badiou, Foucault, Deleuze, and Esposito: In Between the Ruler–Ruled Relation of Political Power? 19
    Alain Badiou on the Event, and the Possibility and Impossibility of Impasse 22
    Foucault, Resistance, Subjectivation, and the Overcoming of a Temporary Impasse 28
    Gilles Deleuze and the Impasse of the Societies of Control 40
    Roberto Esposito, Impasse, and the Immunological Paradigm of Political Life 47
    Resistance in Immunity: Life, Person, and the Impersonal 51
    As Long as There Is Life, There Is Hope and the Possibility of Resistance? 58
    Possibility in the New Political Impasse 64

3 Impasse and the Recovery and Transformation of Selfhood 73
    Recovery of a Zone of Selfhood That Is *Our* Own: *Oikeiosis* 73

The Emergence of World, the Inner, and Auto-Affection 83
The Manifestation of a World from Within 84
Auto-Affection: The Opening onto the Inner Life 94
Self-Becoming: To Feel and Live Oneself Anew? 107
Thinking 113
How Does Thinking Affect Political Impasse? 117
Imagination 119
Judgment 124
Willing 127
Newness and the Inner Turn 130
Communifying Possibility and Hope 141
The Experience of the Initial Possibility of Freedom 147
Dilating the Time of Impasse from Within 148
The Possible Present: A Threshold 150
The Time of Being-Held in Being and the Giving of Time 158
Lingering and Security in Being: A Dialectical Relationship? 168

Conclusion: On Possible New Forms of Selfhood 173

Notes 175
Bibliography 188
Index 193

ACKNOWLEDGMENTS

This book would not have been possible without the support of friends and fellow philosophers. I owe a debt of gratitude to Diane Enns, André Oberlé, Paola Melchiori, Steve Lofts, and Gyöngyi Hegedüs. They make possible the life of the mind that Hannah Arendt so passionately sought and lived. I am also hugely grateful for the love and philosophical acumen of Fadi Abou-Rihan. His deep insights and questions have guided and inspired my work. King's University College has generously supported this work and my colleagues have helped refine many of the ideas contained in it. Karen Enns assisted with the editing of this book and her sharp eye helped give form to the text. Eric Aldieri kindly provided me with useful insights and materials. I thank Liza Thompson and the staff at Bloomsbury for their willingness to take on this project, support, and hard work.

THESIS

Power is classically understood as the playing out of relations between the ruler and the ruled, the oppressor and the oppressed. The moment in which no clear-cut delineation of power exists, no determination of ruler and ruled is obvious, can be called political impasse. Received understandings of political power largely ignore the moment of impasse, absorbing it into the *post facto* structural account of domination of and/or the resistance to an oppressive force. The new neoliberal globalized world has produced a real shift in how power works: not only is power concentrated in the hands of very few while many millions become more oppressed by radical shortages and growing costs, but it is clear that a category in which many find themselves neither rulers nor radically oppressed has emerged. Those who live this neither/nor of contemporary power live impasse. What exactly is impasse and how does it configure itself within or against the understanding of political power is the question that drives this essay in political theory. For those who live in a state of paralysis, compelled to wait for the either-or logic of dominant-dominating powers or practices to break—the results of which are uncertain—this book uncovers possibilities for action in thought, imagination, and self-appropriation through practices of *oikeiosis*, that is, making oneself at home in oneself, and of building constancy. Impasse can be a moment of political self-becoming through affect and thought.

PREFACE

Traditional Western notions of political power generally do not account for impasse as a real, genuine, theoretical moment. Rather, it is considered a form of stagnation or a maintenance of the status quo: There is no clear victor or ruler. Neither people nor objects nor situations seem to change or move, and as no clear outcomes are achieved, an impasse is generally viewed as unproductive, the cause of widespread frustration and irritation within the affected population. Though impasse has been and is still recognized as a historical political event or state, it is largely an undertheorized moment of political thought. Strategically speaking, an impasse may sometimes be desirable as a way of preventing what is considered a far worse or less beneficial situation, but, at best, it may be seen as having a katechonic function: it staves off or holds back more decisive and determining political scenarios.

Power is largely understood in two ways. First, Greek philosophy and science understood it in agential terms, as an action or a capacity to do or enact something, to bring something about, to change one state of affairs into another one. We find this notion of power in such foundational concepts as cause (*aitia*), law (*nomos*), origin (*arche*), act (*energeia*), and potentiality (*dynamis*). Second, there is political power, and it is defined as the rule or dominance of one party over another. Roman power, for example, was conceived as the sovereign power of the ruler to decide who lives and who dies. For Machiavelli, the prince was the conqueror who had vanquished and subdued his enemies, either potential or actual. Even Michel Foucault, who sought to loosen the direct causal structure and immediate agency associated with modern forms of power, for example, pastoral or sovereign power, grasped that though power may be conceived simply as multiplex action upon action, it is marked nonetheless by an oppressive force that encounters various sites of resistance. For the militant and passionate Foucault, impasse or the inability of action to act upon action is seemingly impossible. Power always contains the possibility of resistance, but the outcome of such resistance can be either positive or negative. Foucault cannot think the moment of the being in-between actions, a moment in which no action upon action, especially externalizing action, can occur.

Given the unprecedented geopolitical shifts we have witnessed over the last twenty years, we have to ask: Does our established form of global neoliberal political economic rule simply repeat the classic dynamic forms of the ruler–ruled, or does it make evident what I call political impasse? I think we have to admit the possibility of both options. It is unquestionable that the reduction of politics to economic and market forces has resulted in mass migration, unprecedented environmental damage, the exploitation, violence, and the torture and murder of human beings. The exploitation of textile workers from the Global South by wealthier consumers, factory owners, and distributors to feed the insatiable desire for cheap and disposable clothes in developed countries has caused hardship and death for millions of workers.[1] Here, the wealthy exploit the poor, thereby reinforcing the classic concept of power as the relation between the ruler and the ruled. In her work on populism, Chantal Mouffe tries to recover a robust and empowering concept of populism by exploring the binary of oppressor/oppressed embedded in the Gramscian idea of hegemony and the historical bloc. She writes:

> We can speak of a "populist moment" when, under the pressure of political or socioeconomic transformations, the dominant hegemony is being destabilized by the multiplication of unsatisfied demands. In such situations, the existing institutions fail to secure the allegiance of the people as they attempt to defend the existing order. As a result, the historical bloc that provides the social basis of a hegemonic formation is being disarticulated and the possibility arises of constructing a new subject of collective action—the people—capable of reconfiguring a social order experienced as unjust.[2]

We must concede that not all suffering and oppression are the same, even within the aforementioned dynamic of hegemonic rule and domination brought on by neoliberalism. Some of the population suffer more than others, and gravely so, depending on the relations and differences between classes, gender, ability, and race. The suffering caused by political rule and oppression is subject to the intersectionality that thinkers like Kimberlé Crenshaw and Chandra Talpade Mohanty discuss in their important work.[3] We must note, to further complicate matters, that neoliberalism has been successful in establishing an extra-national and extra-sovereign framework of power. Most citizens of globalized Western countries are not only subjected to their elected governments but also to non-elected international financial and corporate forces that form and run global economies. For citizens who expect direct, democratic representative rule, this results in a form of mass alienation. For example, individuals who participate in our local democracies have little say in the price of food and goods, the cost of energy resources, and interest rates. These market-driven costs, which are so vital for our material existence, are established in complex ways tied to global trends, expectations, futures, and markets. The materials and resources that sustain life are not fully in the grasp of our local elected governments.[4] Mouffe observes:

> As a result the role of parliaments and institutions that allow citizens to influence political decisions has been drastically reduced. Elections no longer offer any opportunity to decide on real alternatives through the traditional "parties of government." The only thing that post-politics allows is a bipartisan alternation of power between centre-right and centre-left parties. All those who oppose the "consensus in the centre" and the dogma that there is no alternative to neoliberal globalization are presented as "extremists" or disqualified as "populists."
>
> Politics therefore has become a mere issue of managing the established order, a domain reserved for experts, and popular sovereignty has been declared obsolete. One of the fundamental symbolic pillars of the democratic ideal—the power of the people—has been undermined because post-politics eliminates the possibility of an agonistic struggle between different projects of society which is the very condition for the exercise of popular sovereignty.[5]

The rise of global financial capitalism and international corporatism, driven in part by thinkers of the Chicago school who deeply feared the centralizing and totalitarian rule of "socialist" [read Marxist] models of economic thought, has introduced a new political order that has strongly reconfigured the way power plays itself out within traditional Liberal states. The voting public, regardless of party affiliation, has little influence over economic policy, which is largely determined outside the political arenas of local parliaments and representative bodies. We have moved beyond the nineteenth- and twentieth-century nation-state model of political economy in which states have greater control over their respective economies and, hence, the resources to manage and execute their own political wills. Currently, business and finance lie for the most part outside the control of governments and voting publics: their institutions and conventions have accumulated enough financial power to significantly influence and structure government policy, both internationally and locally, but they themselves are no longer under the direct auspices of government and the people who elect them. Loosely regulated when compared to other government institutions—especially through instruments of legal and international incorporation—major international agencies of finance and business fall between the legal cracks of international and national borders. Furthermore, powerful global regulating bodies can make direct interventions in sovereign states' economies. One thinks of the recent and ongoing efforts of the World Bank and the International Monetary Fund to dictate national economic policy in Greece, Ireland, Spain, Portugal, and Italy.

Western Liberal government, understood to maintain rule by law while protecting citizens' property rights, withdrew or was evacuated from economics after the collapse of the welfare state in the 1970s, only to have business and financial giants reconfigure the will and desire of government as the neoliberal individualized "competition to protect."[6] The dependency of government on neoliberal financial capital has produced a situation in which the people no longer truly determine their own state; rather, it is determined by the agenda of the new, all-pervasive, global financial machine. No matter what state-sanctioned mechanisms we use to change our politics, we still find ourselves under the crushing demands of global financial markets and institutions. Politics serves, indeed, has become, the economy, which is neither accessible nor participative nor equal for all citizens. The will of the people no longer determines the politics of a state: the people, understood as a formal, political body, have become powerless, mere cogs stuck in the new machine of global markets controlled by the few. Here, we find ourselves again in the traditional playing out of power understood as the rule of a few over the many, whether within an oligarchy or kleptocracy.

But this massive paradigm shift has also created a sense of impasse: There are vast numbers of people living in Western democracies who neither feel the oppression of local and global rule (indeed, they may inadvertently collude with it to some extent) that certain poor and marginalized groups and individuals violently and desperately do, nor have the power to respond in any meaningful or concrete way that can bring about significant change or reform. Whatever they do, individually or collectively, simply fizzles out or is katechonized, to borrow an expression from Carl Schmitt and Roberto Esposito—all attempts at transformation are absorbed by the powers that be, thereby neutralizing and limiting any possible impact of a move for change. The status quo is preserved, staying off any significant, real change. These individuals find themselves in a political impasse, for they cannot be fully identified with the subjected or with the rulers, even though they participate fully in government and society with all the rights accorded to citizens by law.

The individuals of the new neoliberal impasse have benefited from the unprecedented generation of capital and profit, and the opportunities it brings, either through investment or work: they generally do not lack the material necessities of existence such as food, housing, security, and financial stability. In fact, they are materially comfortable. An example of one living in the new form of impasse is the average, middle-class worker-citizen of a Western democracy, who, as a member of a class of society, is gradually being absorbed into the body of the oppressively ruled. These individuals, oppressed by the same system that has made them comfortable, are aware of the needs of those who truly suffer and want to help. But apart from expressions of solidarity and moments of giving monetarily to help improve the lives of those excluded or marginalized, deep structural political reform remains impossible.

Unlike the urban and working poor of our great cities, the refugees, the mentally and physically ill, the racialized and the ghettoized minorities, the precariat of the gig economy, some students and temporary faculty, etc., the worker-citizens caught in the impasse actively participate in government elections, but their vote lacks real clout to make significant change as it does not affect forces outside the limited domain of politics; they have no true access to change the political forces that lie beyond their own systems of sanctioned rule. They vote and participate in legitimate constitutional governments, but they do not have any real access to change the political forces and doings of those that lie beyond or behind their own systems of sanctioned rule. Any potential power these individuals might have is blocked or neutralized by the rulers who control the vast material and economic resources that sustain life and ground politics at the international and local levels. They are allowed to vote only on matters that do not impede or change the dominant superstructure of global financial capitalism.

Marginalized individuals and groups in society, however, remain excluded from participation because of the demands and prejudices of dominant economic classes (one should add here also dominant racial and gendered groups); they are subjectivated or *asujetti*, to use Foucault's term. The impassed configure a new subjectivity that, on one hand, participates in legitimate Liberal state government, but, on the other, cannot access the deeper structure of rule that conditions the very shape of governmental direction and ideological commitment.

A political impasse may be overcome either by a turn of events or by a random change in the status of citizens directly impacted. One may, for example, become part of the ruling elite or, sadly, become confined by the political situation in which one finds oneself. But what do we do when we find ourselves stuck in a political impasse, forced to wait for some release or resolution? More precisely for our purposes here, What can thinking do in times of political impasse?

The pressure of living in a seemingly hopeless impasse constrains us to think otherwise; much like Plato's *aporia*, the impasse forces a turn inward, providing us a critical opportunity to see and reimagine our subjectivation. We can think differently about our situation and envision a new form of politics, a new way of being together. To think otherwise is an expression of human freedom insofar as we can become aware that the necessity of a given moment of impasse is neither eternal nor absolute. Moreover, thinking of new possibilities restores a kind of agency: the possibilities are given to us in thought. To think otherwise is a crucial power, and it can be cultivated through a sustained examination of the encounter between active thought and its more enduring repository in the inner self. Thought alone is not, however, enough to bring about tangible and imaginative response to political impasse. The imagination is needed to extend the possibilities that arise in thinking otherwise; it allows us to see newness that stems from realizing that, indeed, we can think otherwise. The imagination gives these possibilities new shape, a reworked quality, or even a slight modification of form.

But the imagination is not only active as it brings forward new images and ideas. It has a passive aspect to it: imagination affects us. It indicates which prospects are more interesting to us, which possibilities we care more about. In many ways, the affect of the imagination incites desire and may create the psychic energy that allows these envisioned possibilities to emerge with differing intensities. As a result, we must employ judgment to distinguish the variations born in thought we must evaluate which ones to follow and which ones to abandon. In willing, we choose between the differing intensities, push them to completion, and translate them into action.

One might object: but do people not think otherwise in the traditional power structure of ruler and ruled? Did not the oppressed and marginalized of New York respond to and resist the financial crisis of 2008 with the Occupy Movement? Did not large global financial institutions work to save certain corporations that were too large, too important to fail, and all with impunity? Have not global leaders and scientists worked together, scientifically, economically, and politically, to combat COVID-19?

What, then, is unique about thinking in an impasse? The individual living in impasse feels frustrated and hopeless, though perhaps not completely oppressed. The difference in impasse is the affective dimension, which produces unique feelings that indicate a certain state of mind (*Befindlichkeit*, in Martin Heidegger's language), including guilt, ressentiment, helplessness, and complicity. Friedrich Nietzsche tells us these feelings mean we must think and be otherwise in the in-between of a seeming possibility of action clouded in impossibility. Yet, the effect of feeling stuck in political impasse can be deeply influenced by thinking, for, as Marcus Aurelius shows us, our own thinking can be self-transformative. Thinking is not simply a question of calculation, deduction, reasoning, or judgment; it is also an affect which can move us to quell and limit the effects of impasse. To think otherwise is one way, albeit not the only way, to cultivate possibility.

In short, impasse is a state of political being, and it creates a new subjectivity marked by an affective dimension of seeming hopelessness triggered by the seeming ineffectual capacity of action upon action to change the deeper material and ideological oppression of a dominant system of rule that operates outside the recognized form of state rule and sovereignty. In impasse, externalized or externalizing actions are ineffective, though perhaps only temporarily so. In times of impasse, we may turn inwards to help undo dominant subjectivation by creating or launching the possibility of other, new forms of subjectivity inspired by novel and creative ways of thinking and being. One important resource in times of impasse is a genuine turning inward that may create or launch the possibility of new forms of subjectivity that can undo the strictures that make us subject to the new form of impasse.

1

The New Impasse

Deeper Conditions of the Contemporary Impasse: The Fatigue of Forms of Change and the Rise of a New Form of Political Impasse

Political impasses have always existed. As moments of political power, though, they are usually swept into the post facto historical accounts of the clear determinations of events that follow them. An impasse between two sides in conflict, for example, is usually understood according to the dominant interest of the parties involved and narrated to show some kind of victory or benefit. We see this clearly when we examine the twentieth-century wars in Korea, Vietnam, and Afghanistan: the moment of impasse is absorbed by the more defining determinations of victory and loss or ruler and ruled. If there is something like a new form of political impasse, we have to account for the inability on the part of a group to bring about significant political change. All political change is historically conditioned. But it is not only the advent of neoliberalism, with all of its contradictions, that is responsible for the current structure that makes manifest yet another moment of impasse. Part of our inability to move beyond the impasse, which political theorist Chantal Mouffe indicates is the result of the failed response of neoliberal economics to deal with the ensuant collapse of 2008 that produced noxious forms of populism,[1] lies in the fact, I claim, that our political imaginary has been deeply conditioned by two once very successful paradigms of change: reform and revolution.

Rosa Luxemburg brilliantly distills the power (and impotence) of these two paradigms of change in her famous work *Reform or Revolution?*.[2] She mines the historical development of socialist reformists, as well as their contemporary defense of the possibility of change through the adoption of proposed Liberal (and capitalist) reforms sanctioned by both government and the rule of law, and ultimately rejects this approach as either affirming an unjust and oppressive status quo or being slow and inefficient. Luxemburg favors revolution, and she justifies her case through economic and historical analysis. The question that haunts her concerns timing—when to launch a revolution?—as both historic and economic considerations do not yield an exact answer. She emphasizes the need to pay close attention to the conditions that make revolution possible. Some would argue that, sadly, Luxemburg misjudged her own time, evidenced by her own failure (and brutal death) to bring about revolutionary change in the German Revolution of 1919. What is profoundly interesting about Luxemburg's thought is the deep awareness of history and the way in which it conditions material reality.

History, or historical consciousness, becomes increasingly rich as it collects and ponders the thoughts and deeds of humans while constantly offering interpretations and insights about them in their present situation. It sheds light on crucial aspects of human activity, especially politics. When we examine the history of political thinking, we certainly find a plethora of ideas that have become stagnant, violent, or noxious, such as the totalitarian philosophies of National Socialism, Fascism, and Soviet Communism. Indeed, most political theory has as its motivating impetus a series of circumstances and a number of political personalities that have failed miserably at achieving any kind of politics aimed at human flourishing: Plato responds to the crisis of the Thirty Tyrants, Thomas Hobbes to the civil wars, and Hannah Arendt to totalitarianism and capitalist consumer societies. Political thinkers offer alternatives and solutions to what they see as the decadence of political rule. We must acknowledge that some of what is offered is plainly impractical or shortsighted, and some is unacceptable on account of its inherent inhumanity—it simply breeds violence and enforces divisive practices.

We can certainly read the history of political thinking as a response to crisis, but even so, such an understanding ascribes to the agents and events involved in any historical situation either the capacity and power to respond or the freedom and willingness to respond to given circumstances. Change, it seems, is always possible in the sense that we can change the balance in the ruler–ruled dynamic.

Plato's *Republic*, for example, is a response to what he sees as a decadent and corrupt Athens suffering from the legacy of the Thirty Tyrants. His vision of a new polis is illumined by the Good—the philosopher-king not only sees the forms, but also the Good. Society is ordered according to different classes of people that justly carry out what they are by nature designed to do as rulers, guardians, or workers. Plato unabashedly defends a hierarchy of political power and no one escapes the ruler–ruled relationship that he establishes among the classes. All classes are bound by the demands of justice; the philosopher-king is subject to the truth of the forms and the Good. Some would argue Plato's republic is tyrannical because the philosopher-king is conceived of as the summit of power with full illumination while other classes are purposefully and maliciously denied certain knowledge, as evidenced by the famous myth of the metals, and Plato's insistence on the need for what some have called the noble lie: the classes, ultimately, need to work as one if the new polis is to thrive, and this involves the execution of the ruler–ruled relationship.

Medieval thinkers, drawing from Plato and the Neo-Platonists, also see power as the relation between the ruler and the ruled. Whether we speak of Dante's defense of rule by the one, namely, monarchic rule, or Marsilius of Padova's firm division between papal power and the power of the Holy Roman Emperor, ultimately, all are subject to God. Medieval political power introduces into Western thinking an absolute, natural order that is intimately connected to the God of monotheism. This God, the one being who is exempt from the dynamic of the ruler and ruled, is subject to no one and subjects all. The exemption becomes important in modernity because of the sovereign state of exception: sovereigns are truly sovereign because they can exempt themselves from the rules of state, a claim reserved only for God.

Machiavelli and Hobbes, two important initiators of modern political thought, claim that sovereign rule can discipline and bring order to a world tragically suffused with the darker shades of human nature. Machiavelli notes that politics is born out of the need to try and control human volatility and fickleness, whereas Hobbes believes humanity to be in a state of constant aggression; *homo homini lupus*, "we are to each other as wolves," he tells us. Yet, in each of these modern models of politics, whether the Leviathan of government, the prince, or a reworked Roman model of republican rule—and though some form of sovereignty is asserted by rulers in these models—rule is still understood as a relationship between a ruler and the ruled. Machiavelli and Hobbes painstakingly detail the ways in which rulers are dependent on their subjects, and how they should avoid civil strife and tyrannical models of rule that will inevitably and miserably fail, as did the reign of Agathocles. We know that both philosophers lived in times of protracted civil unrest and sought stability through new models of rule that promised the peace and security vital for human flourishing.

Though many Western governments have modern forms of political rule, for example, the checks and balances in place among different branches of government, and rule by law, I believe we are no longer just modern subjects. Michel Foucault's analyses of power show us how it can manifest itself in a plethora of ways, and not only in material ones; nonetheless, he views power as structured by relations between a dominant and subjectivating force. Foucault succeeds in showing, through his careful and expansive studies of documents, archives, disciplining practices, especially on the "cellular" or granular levels, that power need not be framed simply as a series of direct, traceable, and immediate actions caused by an agent. He loosens the connection between actor and agent to show how institutions, human beings' relations, and bodies configure themselves in visible and invisible relations of power. Power is ubiquitous. Although traditional concepts of power root it in an individual such as God, a prince or monarch, government, or the people, Foucault's understanding brings a unique dimension to the evolution of the concept. Political change, then, need not be centered only around the removal of traditional holders or causal nexuses of power. Often when such leaders and centers of power are eliminated, the problems remain, albeit in different forms. Political change and resistance, Foucault shows us, can come from different directions and result in varying structures: political change is a multilateral possibility.[3] Power and change have become more complex phenomena following the intensification and complexification of contemporary global society; older models of change marked by the removal of key actors are no longer sufficient.

Furthermore, the ascendency of a new global financial order, the explosion of technology and communication-information networks, and an unprecedented growth in the human population have created a new political order which lays the groundwork for how we view power and political change. Zygmunt Bauman calls this new reality liquid modernity[4] or, simply, globalization. He observes that the establishment of a new, looser and less centralized, neoliberal financial capitalist order means that traditional forms of government are subject to market demands in ways and on a scale never witnessed before. Elected governments are mobilized not so much by the desires of their citizens, but by the demands and pressures of global capitalism. People thus become alienated, subject to rule that does not stem from their own local governments, understood as structures of rule. People are subject to rule that does not stem from their own traditionally centralized and territorially bounded governments, but from international and global forces, including competition, trade deficits, IMF and World Bank policies, and massive and complex global supply chains. Noam Chomsky discusses the ascendancy of this new political, global financial rule that operates outside the borders of both national and international sovereignty, thereby giving to it greater flexibility of movement and unchecked freedom to exert the force necessary to achieve its own goals.[5]

Today, with the ascendency of financial capital oligarchies and nationalist regimes, such as Victor Orban's Hungary, we have a firmly established form of rule that has eclipsed the power of legitimately elected governments to change the course of events within their own states. Christian Marazzi quotes Antonio Negri in his discussion of the foregoing shift:

> The sovereign government on national territory, writes Negri, "hasn't worked for decades: to reestablish an effectiveness it uses a procedure of *governance*. But this, too, is insufficient—the same local government needs something that goes beyond a territorial state, something that substitutes the exclusive sovereignty that the nation-state otherwise possessed." The passage from government as the state modality of the regulation of growth to governance as the exercise of technocratic control—partial, punctual and local—is exactly what we have been witnessing in the international crisis of sovereign debt. It isn't by chance that the financial crisis is, *de facto*, a banking crisis, an insolvency crisis in which regional banks, from the German *Landesbanken* to the Spanish *Cajas* to nation states and American cities, find themselves on the brink of bankruptcy, struggling to reduce their debts.... Today, international financial

markets are the ones that, with the "simple" differential of bond revenues, technically determine if a citizen of Greece, Illinois or Michigan has the right to retirement funds or if he or she has to resort to public assistance to survive.[6]

Marazzi remarks that the new financial capitalism can move and shape the lives of masses of people in unprecedented ways. He observes:

> Analyzing financial capitalism under this productive profile means talking about *bio-economy* or *bio-capitalism*, "whose form is characterized by its growing connection to the lives of human beings. Previously, capitalism resorted primarily to the functions of transformation of raw materials carried out by machines and the bodies of workers. Instead, bio-capitalism produces value by extracting it not only from the body functioning as the material instrument of work, but also from the body understood as a whole." (Vanni Codeluppi, *Il biocapitalismo. Verso lo sfruttamento integrale di corpi, cervelli, emozioni* (Torino: Bollati Boringhieri, 2008))[7]

Christian Lotz adds to the insights of Marazzi by observing that the abstraction caused by a reduced quality of life—so much time and effort is involved in the basic exchange mechanism of money—has led to the impoverishment of the human spirit, and ultimately created a culture of tutelage in which the financially powerful rule over the masses.[8] Furthermore, as the Italian philosopher Maurizio Lazzarato argues, global financial capitalism has produced a new class distinction between debtors and creditors,[9] in which the latter oppresses the former. The most recent financial collapse of 2008 has left many countries, including Greece, Spain, Portugal, Ireland,

Cyprus, and Italy, in dire economic circumstances. The International Monetary Fund (IMF) and various national central banks demand austerity measures and countries comply, for they are reliant upon hefty bailouts to prevent the collapse of their internal economies. Citizens are then forced to accede to imposed salvage plans and pay from their own private funds, as they did in Cyprus to support the local banking system. And as Elettra Stimmili argues, the economy of widespread debt and austerity has reinforced age-old logics of sin and justified punishment aimed at controlling and limiting the lives of countless individuals.[10]

The varied responses to the 2008 crisis are fascinating, but the majority, in my view, are framed in a reworked late-nineteenth-century paradigm of revolution that has been filtered through the politics of the 1960s. I believe such paradigms have become largely ineffective; they do not bring about any major changes or, at least, the major structural changes they demand. Movements like *Idle No More* and *Occupy Wall Street* started off with great support and hope, but dissipated over time, revealing, in the end, a lack of any perduring unifying force that could effectuate real and long-lasting change. The status quo of neoliberal financial capitalism remains.

There are many reasons for such short-lived, ineffective responses, including the changing nature of power, as mentioned above, media representation, the nature of our limited consciousness and attention, material and financial resources, the impact of technology and media, power divisions, human greed, and human desire, but one of the major reasons is overlooked: the very responses we have formulated are heavily dependent on ideological or conceptual forms of change that are gravely fatigued, namely, revolution and Liberal reform (both with their strategies of disobedience, protest, and violence). It would be fair to say that our notions of political change are deeply colored by the historical framework in which we situate change. Let us recall that not all historical political changes are the same: each one is relative to its time and is understood within the conceptual apparatus of its time. For instance, Plato did not wish to speak of change proper, but rather, the truth of conforming to the demands of the eternal—the good, true, and beautiful. As an Athenian Greek, he understood reality to be eternal, and called for a conversion of thought (*periagoge*) at a time when political thinking was unable to take in the eternal forms and citizens were unable to live according to them. Constant change (i.e., becoming) is, for Plato, a thing to be avoided and, at least in some of his writings, a serious source of disease insofar as it inhibits human flourishing.

Today, the French philosopher Alain Badiou could be said to be one of the leading thinkers of revolution or what he calls the "event."[11] He is the living synthesis of nineteenth-century Marxist-inspired revolutionary politics, Maoist sensibilities, and 1960s' student-worker politics. Badiou is the true *soixcentehuitard*. He teaches that genuine politics happens only when there is a radical rupture of a given political order driven by state oppression. The rupture is truly an event when the situation is reordered by the very event that brings it about. A new subjectivity and new sense of time emerge with the decision on the part of the actors involved to bring about revolutionary change. Badiou gives us examples, including the French Revolution, the Russian Revolutions, and May 1968. Needless to say, what qualifies as an event is monumental in scope. The French Revolution, for example, marked the end of the very possibility of divine absolutist monarchical rule;

the totalizing reigns of Louis XVI and his predecessor, Louis XIV, would never again be possible.

But the political conceptual framework of revolutionary events has become tired, despite what Badiou argues. Why? People have lost faith in this conceptual apparatus. The revolutionary promise of Marxian-inspired regimes like the former Soviet Union, Cuba, and China led, in reality, to brutal systems as corrupt and abhorrent as the previous imperial and capitalist regimes. The promised economic well-being, which would allow human desire to flourish according to the needs and means of each individual, was not delivered. Hierarchies were enforced, and the collapse of these regimes or their transformations into huge capitalist world powers, as in the case of China, renders impotent revolution as an effective model of change.

In Western Liberal economies, on the contrary, the demands for social change or reform articulated in the 1960s by great civil leaders like Martin Luther King Jr., Gloria Steinem, and Harvey Milk produced revolutionary change for African Americans, women, gays, and lesbians. Governments and courts responded by extending rights and protections to vast segments of populations that were previously limited or excluded from participating fully in civil society. In many ways, the spirit of the 1960s still animates the desire for change and equity. Yet, despite these great social and political changes, the framework or paradigm of revolutionary change is no longer effective in Western Liberal democracies. Change is brought about through the traditional mechanisms of the democratic vote, the court system, and the legislative process—all instruments of reform. With greater access to these mechanisms, the need for revolutionary change has quelled. We can use the system to bring greater equity and peace, and we have at our disposal the courts, legislators, the media, and freedom of expression—or so the argument goes.

Equality unfolds through a process of Liberal reform rather than through revolution, and, for many, the social and political situation has improved with the extension of equal rights. But more forceful than the impact of achieved reforms has been the operation and effect of the general intellect of capitalism, or what is now called semiocapitalism, which inevitably cannibalizes and easily assimilates all reforms, ultimately muting their impact and preserving the status quo of gross inequity between the 1 percent at the economic apex and the rest.

Karl Marx, in the *Grundrisse*, describes the general intellect as the working together of technology and social intellect to alter the very nature of work, production, value, and so on, the very being of humans. Franco Berardi notes that advances in technologies have produced new forms of work and products that are no longer purely material. Financial capitalism produces wealth derived from a vast complex of relations that are not necessarily rooted in material realities; the work it demands requires workers to use, sell, and exchange their minds and spirits, understood as the power of their uniquely situated freedoms. This results, ultimately, in forms of abstraction and alienation that come to have deleterious effects on human beings. Berardi remarks:

> Digital technologies open a completely new perspective for labor. First, they transform the relation between conceiving and executing, and therefore the relation between the intellectual contents of labor and its manual execution. Manual labor is generally executed, automatically programmed machinery, while innovative labor, the

one that effectively produces value, is mental labor. The materials to be transformed are simulated by digital sequences. Productive labor (labor producing value) consists in enacting simulations later transferred to actual matters by computerized machines. The content of labor becomes mental, while at the same time the limits of productive labor become uncertain. The notion of productivity itself becomes undefined: the relation between time and quantity of produced value is difficult to determine, since for a cognitive worker every hour is not the same from the standpoint of produced value.[12]

Berardi notes that financial capitalism kills the spirit and the power of free thinking in workers, as well as their capacity to imagine themselves freely and free.

The implications of spiritualization, for example, cognitive work, mean that capitalism, especially financial capitalism, is conscious of itself and can act to stem any threats to its existence; it will use the tenets of liberal democracy, such as freedom of expression and judicial reform, to its own advantage. The economic collapse of 2008 ushered in a series of banking reforms proposed by various democratic legislative and judicial institutions that were supposedly meant to address questions of economic justice and retribution for losses and harms incurred. Yet, we still have the 1 percent issue of gross social and economic inequality. Most of the individuals and firms behind the collapse of 2008 remain unpunished for the reckless hedging and willful overextension of capital and futures. In addition, current capitalist institutions, such as banks, deploy media to justify their actions, even creating pop-paraphernalia like T-shirts and billboards—they market themselves as convenient friends who will help their customers achieve the Liberal dream of home, entertainment, and a leisurely retirement. Banks have become the avid supporters of cultural and charitable organizations, and great Liberal causes like equal rights for the LGBTQ community. We even find various NGOs, whose sole motive is financial gain, espousing revolutionary figures or causes supportive of more Liberal banking policies and the financing of organizations dedicated to enhanced profit. Part of the deep power and strategies of control of neoliberal institutions and practices is to make people believe that there is no way out of an economized rule: the economy is the very material or stuff of life. This no-way out, the artificial necessity of a self-reinforcing economic system, is ideological, no doubt, but it also creates a profound feeling of impasse.

In short, financial capitalism can use any political system to its advantage; it has become conscious of group psychology and the technologies with which to manage it. Any sign of a potential threat is met with the Liberal framework of reform and neutralized. Often, the appearance of concerned reform is given—just enough to stifle any opposition, which usually involves some financial gain for one or more of the injured parties—but deep, structural change does not happen. The status quo and continued commitment to neoliberalism continues, with its heavy emphasis on competition, free markets, and possessive individualism. Semio- and financial-capitalism are marked by a katechonizing self-conscious logic.

In addition to the general historical failure of revolutions to bring about their promised radical changes as the spiritualization of capitalist reform, there has been a loss of faith in the 1960s' generation, many of whom are our leaders—the baby boomers, the supposed actors of the revolution or social reform. Many have turned out to be "Cadillac socialists" or, in the words of Marxist thinkers, bourgeois revolutionaries: they preach revolution and change, yet they live extremely comfortable bourgeois existences. The solidarity between citizens of a classless society has not materialized. It is not uncommon to find top CEOs, once proponents of 1960s' revolutionary ideals, have found that life is made more comfortable with the money earned by adopting neoliberal economic politics.

The moral power of the conceptual framework of nineteenth-century revolution filtered through 1960s' civil rights changes has been exhausted, then, for three reasons: the failure of the movement to deliver on its promise concomitant with the brutal lived reality; the neutralizing absorption of the mechanism of revolutionary change by a traditional Liberal apparatus of reform which includes courts, capitalism, and the granting of rights and freedoms; and, finally, the hypocrisy of 1960s' radicals who do not live according to the principles they fought for and championed. The loss of faith and the inability to commit and sustain a revolution is a sign that what Badiou calls fidelity to the event is no longer possible.

But there exists another reason why the revolutionary and reformist models of change no longer work, and this has to do with borders, more precisely, with their transformation into virtual, digital borders. Revolutionary change is only possible when state pressures, usually confined within specific borders and laws, become intolerable. Because the pressures are restricted, people are able to organize and form serious oppositions. Haiti's recent revolution, for example, was possible because power, in the hands of Duvalier and his state apparatus, was limited by the national borders within which he operated.

The new financial global order does not observe the national and geographic borders drawn, for the most part, at the end of the nineteenth and beginning of the twentieth centuries. The material mechanisms and instruments that enforce the order are not confined to these locational or spatial borders. In fact, borders shift and become more porous in various trade agreements and exchange mechanisms that work electronically and digitally and are not centered in any one place. The General Agreement on Trade and Tariffs is one such agreement: individuals are not only beholden to geographic and material political structures, which can maintain some internal stability, but are also dependent on powerful international economic and political bodies that are neither localized nor geographic—corporations in the true and legal sense of the word. I refer to large banks and agencies like the IMF. People in specific countries have limited means, resources, and knowledge—or lack them altogether—to respond to external technological power that ruptures and compels them; they find themselves confined to using the apparatus and conventions of their local states which seem unable to respond to the new international, financial semiocapitalist order. There are few international agencies, if any (the International Court, Interpol?), that operate at the same spiritual speed and have the same material force to compel and resist the semiocapitalist network of financial capitalism. Our national borders have become cages that prevent harm only within the cage; they cannot be defended from outside attacks. Revolution, at least in the way we have conceived of it since the nineteenth century, can only respond to pressures from within the cage. It is impotent against attacks and exploitation that come from outside our geographical and national holding pens.

Christian Marazzi claims that the response to financial crisis has been to look to the past, to try and revive old but once productive models of economic growth. In part, there has been some success at adverting total economic collapse by re-invoking the Keynesian idea of targeted and specific government intervention in the marketplace during times of crisis. But, on the whole, these, too, are nothing short of pipe dreams as he argues:

> The problem is that, analyzed from a distributive point of view (economistic in the last instance), the crisis development of financial capitalism leads to a veritable dead-end. As much as it is thrown out the window, the cliché that finance is parasitic implicitly comes back through the front door. The *impasse*, more theoretical than practico-political, is before everyone's eyes: the impossibility of elaborating strategies to overcome the crisis, the recourse to economic stimulus measures, on the one hand, presuppose the rescue of finance (of which we are really hostages), but, on the other hand, annul the very possibilities of economic revival. Both the right and the left wish for an unlikely return to the real economy, veritable "reindustrializations" of the real economy (preferably a little greener) in order to have a financialized economy that is an accomplice to the destruction of income and employment. But no one worries anymore about describing the nature and functioning of the so-called "real economy." And thus they wish for state aid to industrial sectors suffering from overproduction, aid that is then translated into job and wage deductions, which certainly do not help (on the contrary) to revive the economy as a whole. This urgency to return to "making things" is similar to the psychotic

critique of the supporters of the first industrial revolution: the idea that, unlike land products, "machines do not eat," forgetting that machines also help increase agricultural productivity.[13]

If we accept that our current Western models of response to political crisis are exhausted, what alternative do we have? We have no alternative: we have arrived at an impasse—a moment of political stagnation. No matter what we do or for what we fight, no matter for whom we vote, we are either absorbed into a larger political machine of financial capitalism becoming, therefore, profit-generating, ignored, benign, and/or boring, or we collapse into localized nationalism, war, and anarchy. We seem to be heading toward the latter as we see the dissolution of the colonizing geopolitical configurations of the globe designed by imperial powers.

The space many currently occupy in the new globalized world in which political action or change is made negligible or impossible for those who are neither rulers nor oppressively ruled is a moment of genuine impasse. In impasse, a way forward is not easily imaginable. As Heidegger and Arendt note, genuine thinking occurs when we stand before a nothing that may generate a possibility of a new appearing. The tired tropes of revolution and reform will not help us. They are simply an attempt to relive the past.

2

The Inscription of the Ruler–Ruled Power Relation in Political Thought and the Obscuring of Impasse

Badiou, Foucault, Deleuze, and Esposito: In Between the Ruler–Ruled Relation of Political Power?

Recent reflection on the notion of impasse recognizes its palpable appearance in our social and political lives. Rei Terada argues that "the reality principle of impasse serves to naturalize what Cedric Robinson calls 'the order of politicality': the identification of the politicalorganization of power with social organization as such."[1] Terada compellingly shows through an analysis of the concept of impasse in Hegel and Gramsci that it need not be read simply as a moment of little productivity or as ushering in possible development.

Terada also critiques the recent work of Emily Apter for casting impasse simply as a moment of dominance.[2] Terada rejects the idea that impasse is simply a transitional state determined by an external force, either a dominant power that forces a kind of stagnation or loss of power, or one that holds future liberatory possibilities:

> Figures of impasse both register anxiety about the capacity of political processes that are focalized from within them and magnetize the political organization of society, even casting it as a metaphysically necessary reflection of all there is at times when the supposition that reality is political reality threatens to give way. To imagine different communities, it is possible to forego the figure of impasse as barely productive crisis, just as it is possible and necessary to forego the logic of "development." To the extent that the perception of impasse is a romantic and subaltern recoil from globalization, creating and hoping to inhabit a shelter, it is preferable to the ethos of world spirit, just as political antagonism is vastly preferable to the centralization and homogenization that, Gramsci shows, occupy the center only to transfer it to fascism.[3]

For Terada, the existent discussions of impasse obscure or hide a space that is not reducible to political organization and structuration—a nonworld in which the illusion of a real world of a protectable space is forsaken. Discussions of the impasse and Gramsci fail to recognize that not all of social reality can be politicized. Terada observes:

> Given that world history takes place as real abstraction through all of the processes of coloniality and globalization, at this time there cannot not be politics defended by impasse. But there is not only

that, and not only the attrition and extermination it ominously implies. There is also another non-world, so to speak, that the impasse/breakthrough dynamic renders irreal to the same extent that it makes the political order, the order that created it and the only order it knows, seem like the only reality. Its presence comes forward vividly in the realization that not everyone would be sorry to see the "common ruin" of the lord and the bondsman, as not everyone has been in contention. The "common ruin" of the parties involved in the impasse reads differently, as Luxemburg momentarily reads it, from elsewhere; while waking up outside the political frame might only be the loss of the illusion of a protectable space.[4]

Terada is right to show that Gramscian and Hegelian ideas of impasse are framed within a dialectical logic moved by some foreseeable end, but the claim of the existence of a nonworld is not the only possibility that arises once we strip away the framework of impasse as lodged between the determining logic of power understood as the interplay of rulers and the ruled. As we shall see, the force and pressure of impasse can lead to an oikeiotic recovery of the transformative self.

But can impasse be something other than an unclear boundary between the ruler and ruled or a katechonic strategy? Has not impasse always been an undecided moment of relation between the ruler and the ruled? And is impasse not part of what makes room for the clear definition of the ruler and the ruled? Can there really be an in-between the ruler–ruled relation or state of politics? Given the modern Enlightenment understanding of political freedom and the necessity of change to bring it about, through reform or revolution or both, it is hard to find contemporary theoretical models of political change that reflect on impasse and its possibilities. I would like to explore the thought of the philosophers Alain Badiou, Michel Foucault, Gilles Deleuze, and Roberto Esposito to show how impasse may be a temporary moment of indetermination or indecision or a state of becoming, the "*en route*" to real change, whether positive or negative. These thinkers, so deeply influenced by the modern possibilities of liberation and resistance, pay scant attention to the moment of impasse as a moment of genuine possibility, of an interiority or inward turn that may give rise to a thinking (and being) otherwise.

Alain Badiou on the Event, and the Possibility and Impossibility of Impasse

For Badiou, a revolutionary event is the deliberate, willed, and subjective intervention on the part of an individual or group of individuals that results in a massive shift: the event produces a new regime of being. He delineates four sites of events that bring about such large paradigm shifts: mathematics/science, politics, love, and art/poetry.[5] Though all share a similar structure, they also have unique traits; poetry, for example, has language and ideas as its primary content, whereas love concentrates on intimate human relationships. A political event arises when three specific conditions have been met: first, the state must exert intense pressure on a situation in order to preserve a certain status quo—one can measure the power of the state in relation to the force of the event; second, the political event is collective; and third, the event brings about the destruction of an old form of politics and launches a new form or regime of politics.[6] Here, we are not talking about a routine change of government or leadership; rather, we are talking about a new way of thinking and doing politics. Such changes for Badiou are understood as revolutionary. The conditions he lays out for the becoming of a political event are concrete: events are not a *creatio ex nihilo*. They draw upon a situation that is being severely determined or confined by a particular form of political rule. The reaction against such a pressured political order can be measured retrospectively by the force with which a new regime appears. Obviously, the paradigm Badiou employs for his reading of political events is informed by revolution—the modern revolutions of the eighteenth, nineteenth, and early twentieth centuries. The greater the state of oppression, the greater the reaction. One can understand, then, the intensity of the violence during the French or the American Revolutions as a reaction in kind against the violent oppression of French and English absolutist monarchs. The collectivities that bring about political events create new forms of subjectivity that subjectivize individuals in a new form of self-understanding and being.[7]

An example of such a political event is the French Revolution. The aristocrats and the King, who inherited and embodied a view of monarchy as absolute and identitarian (the monarch is the state), used pressure on their subjects in the form of neglect and exploitation. Led by the likes of Robespierre, Saint-Just, and other revolutionaries, the people acted in unison to overthrow the king and establish a new political order that would render monarchy in its old absolutist form an impossibility—it could no longer arise as a legitimate form of political rule. The citizens would now rule in a new republic which was more inclusive and less autocratic. At least, this was the initial spirit of the Revolution. We know, however, that as it began to unfold, the Terror severely compromised the Revolution's original goals.

In order for an event like the French Revolution to occur, both materiality and a historical situation are required[8]: events gather people and things in a material, historical situation in order to regroup them in a deeply subjectivating fashion. The situation or evental site, described by Badiou as "foundational" (EE 195), is pre-event and consists of a multiplicity that is empty (*vide*) of any individualizing or singularizing force. An event, however, is always located at a point of a situation, that is, it concerns a multiple present (EE 199). The event ruptures a historical situation and becomes a singular site within it (EE 200). Badiou calls the event a site X, a multiple that is composed of the parts of the situation and composed of its own, unique and singular parts (EE 200).

The event of the French Revolution extends, for Badiou, from about 1789 to 1794. It generates a set of various identifying or naming elements, including the electors of the Estates-General, the peasants of the Great Terror, the sans-culottes of the cities, the personnel of the Convention, Jacobins, conscripted soldiers, the guillotine, effects of the tribunals, English spies, the theatre, la Marseillaise, etc. A historian can include in the set "French Revolution" any number of facts that belong to this singular Revolution and not to any other. But the event is not reducible to the collection of facts or elements that belong to the set: they are very much part of the situation that is part of the event, but the event itself exceeds the "inventory" of elements (EE 201). The event of the French Revolution is an ultra-one, *ultra-un*, an axial term that defines and subjectivates a particular consciousness of a time, always in relation to our own time—recall that we can only grasp events in retrospective apprehension (EE 201). Badiou remarks, "Concerning the French Revolution, understood as an event, one must say that it not only presents the infinite multiple of the sequence of facts situated between 1789 and 1794, but it *also* presents itself as an immanent summary and as a unification of its own multiplicity" (EE 201, translation mine). What is unique about any event is the particular subjectivation and temporization that happens: events produce their own singular subjects and times.[9]

The French Revolution produced a new kind of subject and marked a new kind of time. In the case of the former, we see the emergence of a revolutionary subject who seeks to establish a collective political order in which all are equal, despite class, birth, or rank. Examples of *new revolutionary subjectivities* include Rousseau, Saint-Just, and Robespierre. The subject emerges through particular interventions, and the event subjectivates or gives a name to the kind of subject that emerges through the event. In terms of the latter, the French Revolution marks a new historical period: the time of revolutions. Badiou and other thinkers like Antonio Negri admit that the age of revolutions that extended through the twentieth century has become tired,[10] and the call to revolution is often met with apathy or a short-lived burst of energy that does not last more than a few months or weeks. We see this with the Occupy Wall Street movement, for example. So many revolutions have brought about devastating changes and have failed to establish the ideals that inspired them, an outcome which has left many people wary and disillusioned. The age of revolutions can be expanded into a larger set to include other events like the American, Russian, Cuban, and Haitian Revolutions, as well as May 1968.

In general, according to Badiou, there are two kinds of sets or groupings of multiples: those marked by belonging (*appartenance*) and those marked by inclusion (*inclusion*) (EE 95). The first refers to the wide array of multiple elements that can belong to a particular set of elements that constitute a situation, whereas the second refers to the subsets that inextricably belong to a set of a situation. So, within a historical situation such as the French Revolution (recall that the French Revolution is not only an event but also a situation), the three estates (i.e., clergy, nobility, common people) of the Estates-General must be included as part of the Estates-General: there is a necessity attached to the ordering of the subsets of inclusion, whereas with belonging there is an infinite number of multiples that can come to be part of a set. For example, certain laws, ideas, and people may be included in the set of the event called French Revolution, but they were not necessary in order for the French Revolution to be the event that it was. For Badiou, the event itself is held together through time and continues to be meaningful, thereby structuring politics, by virtue of an operation of fidelity on the part of subjects who keep referring back to the event and who are faithful to its singularity. Those faithful to the French Revolution will keep pushing its unique and singular ideas, its singular form of subjectivity, and the spirit of its time throughout future ages. The spirit of the event of the French Revolution certainly lives on in the French Republic today and in many daily customs of the French people. We can also see traces of the French Revolution in the Haitian Revolution of 1986, when Haitians ousted Duvalier after years of abuse, corruption, and violence.

For Badiou, fidelity to an event is conceived as a procedure (EE 257). It is the procedure by which one distinguishes within a situation the multiples whose existence is connected to an event that an intervention brought into action. Fidelity gathers and distinguishes the becoming of that which is connected to the name of the event. It is a kind of referential love: it is also viewed as being very particular (EE 257–258). Fidelity is not a thing; rather, one sees it only by its results; the connections and operation of fidelity are apparent in the effects of the event, especially on time and subjectivity. For example, being faithful to the principles of the American, French, Chinese, or Russian Revolutions will continue to have particular effects in real time and on subjects insofar as these subjects remain faithful to the uniqueness of what these Revolutions name and entail. The current Chinese regime still sees itself as being faithful to Mao's revolutionary principles, though it has substantially reworked Mao's view of agriculture and economics. The education of Chinese students remains rooted in Maoist principles, though some aspects of Mao's originary revolutionary insights have been reformulated because of changing historical and economic situations: other global events such as the rise of global capital and banking networks have shifted the ordering of the elements that constitute the Maoist Revolution.

The aforementioned distinction between the belonging and inclusion of various multiples to a set is important, for it is here that Badiou deploys set theory to loosen the relation of members or elements of a set that constitute an event. Non-necessary aspects of a set may or may not appear in the event as it unfolds. So, the sans-culottes may have been present in the French Revolution of 1789, and they certainly helped define the event, but as the significance and the force of change of the Revolution moved through time, they disappeared. They are not necessary for the later existence of the subjectivating force of the Revolution, just as perhaps Thermidor and Saint-Just are no longer necessary to be faithful to the revolutionary principles of freedom and equality. Set theory allows Badiou to shift and move within relations of belonging and inclusion of the elements that are necessary and/or contingent for the being of an event to unfold, though the event itself is an ultra-one. Determination and indetermination are compossible and, therefore, set up a possibility of seeming impasse as this compossibility is not subject to the traditional logics regulated by the principles of nonsufficient reason and noncontradiction. The life of an event, as it unfolds in time and space, will draw on the foregoing possibility in order to adapt and change to historical circumstances while preserving a core-defining trait, thereby guaranteeing the continued force of political change through time. Yet, what ultimately drives change and our fidelity to a model of political change is the event itself. It has a temporal and subjectivating force. Though Badiou makes room for the compossibility of impasse, it is evenemental as opposed to eventual, that is, impasse is merely an aspect of the general situation, which is still subject to the primacy of the event. Politically, this means that impasse can be understood as a moment or aspect of an event, but it is ultimately superseded by the force of the event itself. Impasse yields some form of possibility, as it makes possible the contingency of choice (decision) and multiplicity of the aspects of an event, but it is not in itself a genuine moment of politics.

Foucault, Resistance, Subjectivation, and the Overcoming of a Temporary Impasse

Michel Foucault, by contrast, understands power as a series of relations that need not be confined to the framework of the event. Political power is a struggle between a dominant force and resisting forces, but power itself must contain the very conditions for its undoing and resistance. If anything, impasse can be a moment within the struggle, but it can never be a constitutive or defining aspect of power itself. Foucault spent his life thinking and rethinking the nature of political power. I cannot undertake here a full exposition of the developments and changes in his richly complex theory, but I do wish to look at two aspects of his understanding of power as relations of force and as subjectivating, in order to show how impasse is marginal to his thinking.

In his famous work, *The History of Sexuality*,[11] Foucault delivers a deeply insightful description of power that displaces the modern agential account. The second chapter of Part Four, "Method," lays the groundwork for an understanding of power as a series of relations that continue to affect people and determine situations even as these effects become increasingly diffuse and extend beyond the traditional logics of causation and attributive agency. The chapter moves from a discussion of the relation between sex and knowledge to sex and power. Power, Foucault argues, is not to be understood in its traditional senses:

> By power, I do not mean "Power" as a group of institutions and mechanisms that ensure the subservience of the citizens of a given state. By power, I do not mean, either, a mode of subjugation which, in contrast to violence, has the form of the rule. Finally, I do not have in mind a general system of domination exerted by one group over another, a system whose effects, through successive derivations, pervade the entire social body. The analysis, made in terms of power, must not assume that the sovereignty of the

state, the form of the law, or the over-all unity of a domination are given at the outset; rather, these are only the terminal forms power takes.[12]

Foucault, following the rich tradition of Marxian thinking, posits that power must be understood as a set of relations of force. These relations operate in a multiplicity of specific realms, and they have their own self-constituting organization. Power does not necessarily operate in a systemic form in which parts relate to one another and a whole; each relation is its own self-organizing realm. Right from the start, Foucault fragments larger and more englobing frameworks of power that are reducible to simple holistic configurations. He elaborates on power as:

> The process which, through ceaseless struggles and confrontations, transforms, strengthens, or reverses them; as the support which these force relations find in one another, thus forming a chain or a system, or on the contrary, the disjunctions and contradictions which isolate them from one another; and lastly, as the strategies in which they take effect, whose general design or institutional crystallization is embodied in the state apparatus, in the formulation of the law, in the various social hegemonies. Power's condition of possibility, or in any case the viewpoint which permits one to understand its exercise, even in its more "peripheral" effects, and which also makes it possible to use its mechanisms as a grid of intelligibility of the social order, must not be sought in the primary existence of a central point, in a unique source of sovereignty from which secondary and descendent forms would emanate; it is the moving substrate of force relations which, by virtue of their

inequality, constantly engender states of power, but the latter are always local and unstable.[13]

Power is to be understood as moving relations of struggle that need not be seen as emanating from a central force. Power, as Gramsci notes, can come from below and may be peripheral—on the margins. Foucault notes that power is omnipresent and is not confined to specific spheres of influence.

> The omnipresence of power: not because it has the privilege of consolidating everything under its invincible unity, but because it is produced from one moment to the next, at every point, or rather in every relation from one point to another. Power is everywhere; not because it embraces everything, but because it comes from everywhere. And "[p]ower," insofar as it is permanent, repetitious, inert, and self-reproducing, is simply the over-all effect that emerges from all these mobilities, the concatenation that rests on each of them and seeks in turn to arrest their movement. One needs to be nominalistic, no doubt: power is not an institution, and not a structure; neither is it a certain strength we are endowed with; it is the name that one attributes to a complex strategical situation in a particular society.[14]

Even when Foucault talks about power being inert, a discussion in which one could read something like impasse, he is quick to indicate this temporary state is always en route to being "arrested," as power moves constantly. Foucault continues to present his conception of power in a series of propositions that follow from the discussion mentioned above.

First, power is not something held or dispersed or shared; rather, it is "exercised from innumerable points, in the interplay of nonegalitarian and mobile relations."[15] Second, it does not occupy an external position vis-à-vis other relations such as sexual, legal, economic, or social ones; it is already immanently at work in all relations, created by the differences, distinctions, inequalities, and hierarchies within them. The power in these relations is productive and is not seen as playing a simple role of prohibition and accompaniment. Third, power "comes from below; that is, there is no binary and all-encompassing opposition between rulers and ruled at the root of power relations, and serving as a general matrix."[16] Fourth, given the omnipresence of the relations of force constitutive of power, the effects of this power are not simply confined to institutions and societal relations such as the family. Power must not be conceived within a top–down or smaller–wider definition. Effects of the relations of force can run through the whole social body, albeit in manifestly variegated forms. Foucault observes:

> One must suppose rather that the manifold relationships of force that take shape and come into play in the machinery of production, in families, limited groups, and institutions, are the basis for wide-ranging effects of cleavage that run through the social body as a whole. These then form a general line of force that traverses the local oppositions and links them together; to be sure, they also bring about redistributions, realignments, homogenizations, serial arrangements, and convergences of the force relations.[17]

Fifth, power relations are both intentional and nonsubjective. Here, Foucault posits that there may exist logics and tactics of power that have specific calculable and rationalizable ends, but that, in their complexity, may not be attributable to a specific agent. One can think of the material force of history that creates certain conditions, which has a directional intentionality traceable in the structure that it shapes but which is not reducible or attributable solely to specific individuals or groups. Finally, Foucault argues that where there is resistance, there one finds resistance, and "this resistance is never in a position of exteriority in relation to power."[18]

The last proposition discussed above raises certain important questions for Foucault that directly touch upon our discussion of impasse. He wonders whether there is no "outside of power," whether we are always in some form of power relations. Can we ever escape power? And if there is no escape, no outside, one could argue we are in a state of genuine impasse. We are stuck in the inevitability of a series of power relations. But Foucault explicitly rejects this possibility of impasse. He writes:

> This would be to misunderstand the strictly relational character of power relationships. Their existence depends on a multiplicity of points of resistance: these play the role of adversary, target, support, or handle in power relations. These points of resistance are present everywhere in the power network. Hence there is no single locus of great Refusal, no soul of revolt, source of all rebellions, or pure law of the revolutionary. Instead there is a plurality of resistances, each of them a special case: resistances that are possible, necessary, improbable; others that are spontaneous, savage, solitary, concerted, rampant, or violent; still others that are quick to compromise, interested, or sacrificial; by definition, they

can only exist in the strategic field of power relations. But this does not mean that they are only a reaction or rebound, forming with respect to the basic domination an underside that is in the end always passive, doomed to perpetual defeat.[19]

Though Foucault disrupts the binary logic of inside and outside, focusing our attention on a sphere of self-organizing domains of power relations that is multiplex and complex, he brings forward a notion of resistance that does not rely on some external relation that will effectuate some change; he looks to the resistance that is already at play within a realm or set of relations. Foucault does admit that some revolutionary change is possible, which is the focus of Badiou's political analysis, but this kind of change is rare, and he certainly would not see it as an ultra-one of the Badiouan event. Foucault is careful to situate resistance and force as co-constitutive of power, and resistance forecloses any genuine possibility of impasse. Though we may resist a force, we are still inscribed within the very dynamic of the relations of force constitutive of power. Struggle is constant. Resistance offers the possibility of a multiplicity of "actions upon actions" within the struggle of power. Impasse, then, is not possible within a Foucaultian understanding of power as relations of force.

But Foucault's understanding of power is not to be reduced to the foregoing account; as he protests in his famous essay "The Subject and Power," his work must not be read to be simply about power but also about subjectivation.[20] How are we turned into subjects? It could be argued that Foucault's analysis of subjectivation shows how one is shaped by subjectivating forces and, therefore, repeats what the embodied form of subjectivation demands. The subjected individual's personal being can be viewed as being in a condition of impasse in which the state of personal being is blocked and unable to form or appear. A Foucaultian subjectivating force creates personal impasse. Yet, the French philosopher is tenaciously committed to offering some way out of these increasingly demanding forms of power, for he continues to insist in the possibility of resistance. Impasse, then, is never a genuine possibility in Foucault's account of subjectivation. If anything, it is a temporary moment within the relation of subjectivating force and resistance. It has no being in and of itself.

How does Foucault build his case for the foregoing claim? "The Subject and Power" begins by noting that all contemporary anti-authority struggles have certain things in common. First, they are traversal, that is, we find them all over the globe. Second, their aim is to tackle the effects of power. Third, they are immediate in the sense that they identify immediate, visible, and direct actors or institutions as targets against which they fight. Fourth, these struggles are all focused on individuals. Fifth, they oppose the effects of power that stem from knowledge, qualification, and competence. And, finally, these struggles revolve around the question: Who are we?[21] If one looks at various anti-authoritarian struggles, from the Yellow Jackets movement to the protests at G-7 meetings, one would be hard pressed to deny the prescience of Foucault's analysis.[22] Foucault notes, however, that such a view of power—as anti-authoritarian struggle—does not fully capture the depth and dynamics of contemporary power. He pushes his readers to think more critically about power. While Foucault grants that contemporary struggles are right to think oppressive forms of power, such as the modern state with its individualizing and totalizing pastoral powers, seek to shape our subjectivity as a means of control over who and what we are, and what we do, how power shapes and subjectivates must not be considered in strictly agential or causal terms:

> The exercise of power is not simply a relationship between partners, individual or collective; it is a way in which certain actions modify others. Which is to say, of course, that something called Power, with or without a capital letter, which is assumed to exist universally in a concentrated or diffused form, does not exist. Power exists only when it is put into action, even if, of course, it is integrated into a disparate field of possibilities brought to bear upon permanent structures. This also means that power is not a function of consent. In itself it is not a renunciation of freedom, a transference of rights, the power of each and all delegated to a few (which does not prevent the possibility that consent may be a condition for the existence or the maintenance of power); the relationship of power can be the result of a prior or permanent consent, but it is not by nature the manifestation of a consensus.[23]

We must ask: What is power? Can it account for impasse? Foucault defines power in the clear and distinct language of relation: "In effect, what defines a relationship of power is that it is a mode of action which does not act directly and immediately on others. Instead, it acts upon their actions: an action upon an action, on existing actions or on those which may arise in the present or the future."[24] Foucault thus clears the field and introduces a notion of power that is constituted by the relations of actions that act upon other actions. Questions of intentionality, motivation, causality, and agency are all displaced in this theory, and the distinction between the internal and external, the inside and the outside of power, is eliminated. A modal structure of power is introduced that emphasizes possibility:

> It is a total structure of actions brought to bear upon possible actions; it incites, it induces, it seduces, it makes easier or more difficult; in the extreme it constrains or forbids absolutely; it is nevertheless always a way of acting upon an acting subject or acting subjects by virtue of their acting or being capable of action. A set of actions upon other actions.[25]

The actions or acts described by Foucault also possess a temporal dimension, as they have potential future effects. Power can direct or lead individuals to act within a certain field of possibilities, but the individual is unable or constrained to think outside the realm of possibilities generated by a subjectivating power:

> Perhaps the equivocal nature of the term "conduct" [*se conduire*] is one of the best aids for coming to terms with the specificity of power relations. For to "conduct" is at the same time to "lead"others (according to mechanisms of coercion which are, to varying degrees, strict) and a way of behaving within a more or less open field of possibilities.[26]

Foucault proceeds to identify five traits of subjectivating power: it is constituted by a series of differentiations; those who act upon the actions of others pursue different types of objectives; power relations are brought into existence by diverse means; there are varied forms of the institutionalization of power and varied apparatuses, from hierarchies to self-enclosed systems, for example; and degrees of rationalization exist as power is brought into being.[27]

Subjectivating power produces a certain subjective form that bears a set of possible expressions and choices, thereby creating a seeming possibility of the subjective will's freedom of choice. But this is only an illusion created by the subjectivation itself. Here, one could argue that we encounter a Foucaultian understanding of impasse insofar as the subjectivity created is limited even by the very possibilities created for it by various powerful actions. But if impasse is to be a truly genuine moment of Foucaultian power, it has to be able to persist. For Foucault, however, one can resist such subjectivating forces. How?

All power relations are embedded in a social world, and the field in which power plays itself out, as we see from Foucault's earlier account of power taken up in *The History of Sexuality*, is as multiplex as it is complex:

> This is not to say, however, that there is a primary and fundamental principle of power which dominates society down to the smallest detail; but, taking as point of departure the possibility of action upon the action of others (which is coextensive with every social relationship), multiple forms of individual disparity, of objectives, of the given application of power over ourselves or others, of, in varying degrees, partial or universal institutionalization, of more or less deliberate organization, one can define different forms of power. The forms and the specific situations of the government of men by one another in a given society are multiple; they are superimposed, they cross, impose their own limits, sometimes cancel one another out, sometimes reinforce one another.[28]

Foucault argues that given this multiplicity and complexity, we must distinguish relations of power from strategies of power. It is this distinction that broadens the definition of power to include within its very structure the concept of resistance. Power, understood as both a relation of force and as subjectivating, can only exist as it has within it the differentiations that are the simultaneously possible sites of resistance to power. Foucault poignantly defines what he means by the term strategy:

> The word "strategy" is currently employed in three ways. First, to designate the means employed to attain a certain end; it is a question of rationality functioning to arrive at an objective. Second, to designate the manner in which a partner in a certain game acts with regard to what he thinks should be the action of the others and what he considers the others think to be his own; it is the way in which one seeks to have the advantage over others. Third, to designate the procedures used in a situation of confrontation to deprive the opponent of his means of combat and to reduce him to giving up the struggle; it is a question, therefore, of the means destined to obtain victory. These three meanings come together in situations of confrontation—war or games—where the objective is to act upon an adversary in such a manner as to render the struggle impossible for him. So strategy is defined by the choice of winning solutions. But it must be borne in mind that this is a very special type of situation and that there are others in which the distinctions between the different senses of the word "strategy" must be maintained.[29]

With the introduction of strategies into power relations, Foucault creates an aperture for resistance endemic to power. No power is absolute, though power is part of the social fabric of society. It is marked by possible reversibility, an insight that plagues the idea of *fortuna* in Machiavelli's *The Prince*, but which Foucault sees as hope. Foucault describes subjectivating power as being characterized by limits that create potential struggle and resistance, thereby limiting the potential force of all power.[30]

Foucault is aware that the claim that escape is always possible elicits significant questions forward. At one point he ponders, raising the possibility of a genuine state of impasse, whether one can remain locked in a constant struggle while one experiences unchanging domination or oppression.[31] Though Foucault admits the real possibility of domination and being locked in a continuous strategic struggle, he concludes his essay by affirming that such struggles are always limits to the force of power and, therefore, represent constant modes of resistance. Even in this later account of subjectivating power, impasse, at best, may be conceived as part of the struggle that constitutes power, an affirmation of it, but it is never given a unique status in Foucault's system. It is not a genuine moment of being blocked, of neither ruling nor being ruled.

Gilles Deleuze and the Impasse of the Societies of Control

Gilles Deleuze greatly admired Foucault's work, but he was also a thoughtful critic. In "Postscript on the Societies of Control," Deleuze pushes Foucault to acknowledge a new political state that has emerged out of the blending of information technology and a newer form of financial capitalism focused on a "higher-order" production.³² The two philosophers were deeply concerned about the rise of neoliberalism and the social and political effects it brought and would continue to bring to the world. The postscript ends with a dire warning to young people—new configurations of technology and higher-order capitalism will create a new master: "Many young people strangely boast of being 'motivated'; they request apprenticeships and permanent training. It's up to them to discover what they're being made to serve, just as their elders discovered, not without difficulty, the telos of the disciplines. The coils of a serpent are even more complex than the burrows of a molehill."³³

Fascinating in Deleuze's engagement with Foucault is the former's intimation of a new impasse in society that advances with the new matrix of information and computer technology and capitalism. How does Deleuze describe this possible impasse? The postscript begins with a recognition of Foucault's great contribution to our understanding of political power through his analyses of disciplinary institutions and societies of the eighteenth and nineteenth centuries. Deleuze notes that Foucault was also astutely aware that such disciplining societies would be surpassed by the idea of the state and its sovereign power. But shifts in society and the advancement of new technologies following the Second World War produced a further development: a society in which both disciplinary and sovereign models of power could no longer account for new modes of power:

> We are in a generalized crisis in relation to all the environments of enclosure-prison, hospital, factory, school, family. The family is an "interior," in crisis like all other interiors—scholarly, professional, etc. The administrations in charge never cease announcing

supposedly necessary reforms: to reform schools, to reform industries, hospitals, the armed forces, prisons. But everyone knows that these institutions are finished, whatever the length of their expiration periods. It's only a matter of administering their last rites and of keeping people employed until the installation of the new forces knocking at the door. These are the societies of control, which are in the process of replacing the disciplinary societies. "Control" is the name Burroughs proposes as a term for the new monster, one that Foucault recognizes as our immediate future. Paul Virilio also is continually analyzing the ultrarapid forms of free-floating control that replaced the old disciplines operating in the time frame of a closed system. There is no need here to invoke the extraordinary pharmaceutical productions, the molecular engineering, the genetic manipulations, although these are slated to enter into the new process. There is no need to ask which is the toughest or most tolerable regime, for it's within each of them that liberating and enslaving forces confront one another. For example, in the crisis of the hospital as environment of enclosure, neighborhood clinics, hospices, and day care could at first express new freedom, but they could participate as well in mechanisms of control that are equal to the harshest of confinements. There is no need to fear or hope, but only to look for new weapons.[34]

The "societies of control" is Deleuze's term for the forces active in the new neoliberal age. Like Gunther Anders, who describes the modern compulsion to build and use new technology, regardless of the consequences, Deleuze notes that in societies of control, there is no specific aim other than to control—to "look for new weapons."

He describes the logic of these societies of control, and like Foucault, claims traditional models of social and political causality and agency are no longer determining. As controls modulate continuously, according to the individuals and circumstances involved, there is greater flexibility and agility. These modulating controls are marked by an indirect logic of analogy, as opposed to that of identification (x is y), thereby undermining the possibility of finding any one source of control. Deleuze notes:

> The different internments or spaces of enclosure through which the individual passes are independent variables: each time one is supposed to start from zero, and although a common language for all these places exists, it is analogical. On the other hand, the different control mechanisms are inseparable variations, forming a system of variable geometry the language of which is numerical (which doesn't necessarily mean binary). Enclosures are molds, distinct castings, but controls are a modulation, like a self-deforming cast that will continuously change from one moment to the other, or like a sieve whose mesh will transmute from point to point.[35]

Deleuze gives the example of the shift from traditional factory work to corporate work. The factory tries to maintain an equilibrium between the lowered costs of production and low wages to gain maximum profit. In order to achieve this, the factory and its workers labor as one body.

But in a society of control, the corporation has replaced the factory, and the corporation is a spirit, a gas. Of course the factory was already familiar with the system of bonuses, but the corporation works more deeply to impose a modulation of each salary, in states of perpetual metastability that operate through challenges, contests, and highly comic group sessions. If the most idiotic television game shows are so successful, it's because they express the corporate situation with great precision. The factory constituted individuals as a single body to the double advantage of the boss who surveyed each element within the mass and the unions who mobilized a mass resistance; but the corporation constantly presents the brashest rivalry as a healthy form of emulation, an excellent motivational force that opposes individuals against one another and runs through each, dividing each within. The modulating principle of "salary according to merit" has not failed to tempt national education itself. Indeed, just as the corporation replaces the factory, perpetual training tends to replace the school, and continuous control to replace the examination. Which is the surest way of delivering the school over to the corporation.[36]

Like Foucault, Deleuze recognizes the fluidity, changeability, and omnipresence of this new form of control. As he describes the concept of the societies of control, he observes that new technologies and machines such as computers, with their passive danger of jamming and their active danger of piracy and viruses, express, like all machines throughout history, "social forms capable of generating them and using them."[37] Big data and the companies that mine and deploy it, for example, Cambridge Analytica, can control the destiny of social and political orders, as witnessed by the presidential victory of Donald Trump in 2016. The intricate and refined targeting of a few voters in swing states was enough to tip the Electoral College in Trump's favor.

Shoshana Zuboff describes how new data technology helps frame a society of control through surveillance capitalism.[38] As technology changed after the Seond World War, so did capitalism. It moved beyond the traditional framework of material production to a more spiritual mode of operation, as discussed earlier, in which buying and selling stocks and futures is as central as buying and selling services. The power of this mode lies in its capacity to transform, disperse, and deform itself.

> The operation of markets is now the instrument of social control and forms the impudent breed of our masters. Control is short-term and of rapid rates of turnover, but also continuous and without limit, while discipline was of long duration, infinite and discontinuous. Man is no longer man enclosed, but man in debt. It is true that capitalism has retained as a constant the extreme poverty of three quarters of humanity, too poor for debt, too numerous for confinement: control will not only have to deal with erosions of frontiers but with the explosions within shanty towns or ghettos.[39]

If Deleuze is right and we find ourselves in a global society of control, we are bound in a continuous and unlimited form marked by quick, short-lived changes—a kind of feedback loop that can be understood as an impasse. But has techno-capitalism, as Deleuze understands it, finally achieved the control he discusses? If we look at his broader corpus, we certainly do not find the structural resistance of Foucaultian power, but we do find possibilities that may undo power, although this is never guaranteed or necessary. The discussion of the rhizomatic versus the arboreal or the royal versus the nomadic or the majoritarian versus the minoritarian in *A Thousand Plateaus*, for example, is meant to show new configurations or intensities of relations and states of affairs may inadvertently undermine dominant forms of power simply by their very being and existing; their own logic evades and is indifferent to dominant and oppressive modes. The nomad is indifferent to the territorial boundaries established and enforced by regal political orders, and simply continues to live as a nomad. Deleuze observes that reality consists of a multiplicity of differentiated logics and ways of being that do not follow the limited orders and regimes established by a specific social and political power. He challenges binary thinking, the either–or of ruler–ruled, for example, by pointing out the deeper structure of reality as marked by difference-in-itself and repetition-in-itself, which constantly multiplies, differentiates, and brings forward new configurations and intensities outside traditional logics of direct causality and agency. The binaries of either–or are replaced by novel forms of synthesis, including the and... and... and... and, which is more adept at dealing with the seeming contradictions of a quantum universe. The implication of Deleuze's ontology is that *per definitionem* any established regime can never be total and all dominant, for life itself has already created the very conditions and possibilities that may undo it: alternative and different systems of being already coexist, so there is always a real outside to any dominant system, an outside that may challenge or be indifferent to the very supremacy of a dominant assemblage.

Impasse, then, may come to exist for Deleuze, but the processes of differentiation and repetition preclude its perdurance. Though we may be stuck in impasse, there is an outside we can look to that may potentially undo it. Roberto Esposito comments on Deleuze's idea of becoming:

> But what is becoming? What must we understand by this term, which plays a decisive role in all of Deleuze's thought? Becoming, for the French philosopher, never refers to a chronological relation between first and after; rather, it is a change determined by the passing from the inside to the outside, for example, to "become animal"; human beings must exit from an anthropocentric model and take on what lies outside the limits of the species. As explained in *A Thousand Plateaus*, against the immunitary tendency to close oneself within the limits of our own species, the becoming animal signifies plurality, metamorphosis, contamination. Again, it is nothing but the outside of that to which we are normally accustomed.[40]

There is a real outside for Deleuze, and philosophy has a significant relation to this outside. In a genuine state of political impasse, one feels, painfully, that there is no outside—the outside cannot penetrate. As we shall see, one must turn within, following the teachings of the sage Stoic philosophers.

Roberto Esposito, Impasse, and the Immunological Paradigm of Political Life

The most significant development in political theory over the past decade is the work of the Italian philosopher Roberto Esposito, whose immunological paradigm challenges Foucaultian biopolitical thought.[41] Can we find in Esposito's thinking a place for impasse as life and death, possibility and impossibility, come to co-constitute one another, thereby setting the conditions for the establishment of a governmentalized ruler–ruler relation while simultaneously planting the seeds for the very undoing of this relation? Though he offers the very concrete hope of resistance and political change within his philosophical oeuvre, impasse has no place within the dynamic movement of the immunological paradigm itself.

As Esposito's thought unfolds, especially in his more recent political work, the pivotal insight gleaned from his studies of Machiavelli on the inherent connection between order and conflict continues to be an influence. For example, in *Immunitas*,[42] Esposito argues that the very structure of biological life, though ordered and shaped by governmentality and political life (following Foucault and Agamben), contains within its being a resistant power that comes into conflict with the growing demands of governmentality and political life, the *bios* of Aristotle. His analysis of the immunitary paradigm, especially within medicine and politics, shows that life itself has the potential (albeit not the necessity) to resist attempts to control and manipulate a reductive biopolitical conception of life. Indeed, resistance has become a key concept for Esposito, evidenced by his claim that one of the unique aspects of Italian modern political theory is the sustained focus on possibilities of resistance. Impacted by life, events, tumult, violence, and struggle, Italian philosophy has always sought ways to resist dominant and oppressive forces in order to create new philosophical possibilities, which often work within the domain of the immunitary paradigm.[43] Order, conflict, resistance—these three concepts run through Esposito's corpus.

A particular challenge posed by Esposito's thought centers around the concept of the human person. Undoubtedly, the person has been and continues to be an important legal concept in Western countries, and the development of human rights in the twentieth century is intimately linked to an understanding of what a person is. The concept of person faces two important challenges. First, its more recent political configuration within human rights discourses, especially after the systematic and horrendous violence and death caused by the Second World War, seems incapable of resisting the increasing violence that marks geopolitics today. In other words, the various human rights declarations drafted and legally instituted over the last sixty years, all designed to enshrine and protect the dignity and rights of human persons through an agreed and shared understanding of what a human person is, have failed to protect millions of people from continued abuse, persecution, violence, and execution. Second, the massive changes already introduced by technology, as well as the envisioned future changes as technology is combined with human life in more complex and dramatic forms, means that the very nature of the human constitutive of the human person becomes questionable: How human are human persons in light of prosthetic, regulative, diagnostic, and enhancing biotechnologies that alter genetic and body structures in order to produce a new technologized being?

The aforementioned challenges contest the nineteenth- and twentieth-century Liberal views of the human person, understood as a rational, free, autonomous, and unified mind–body individual. Esposito has argued in various works, especially in his *Third Person*,[44] that we have to rethink the category of the person. Drawing inspiration from such thinkers as Gilles Deleuze (the notion of the immanence of a life) and Simone Weil (the impersonal), he argues that within the immunitary paradigm of life, there is a zone of biological life that can resist, or that lies outside, our political, governmentalizing, and structuring political forces that wish to dominate and control biological life. As Bergson shows in *Creative Evolution*, the very becoming and force of life itself is not reducible to human control, as life itself, in its becoming, exceeds the limited nature of human knowing and acting precisely because of its evolutionary structure: life evolves and is not finished or complete; it can change, become other, and alter itself in ways we cannot anticipate. Esposito's view of the impersonal alerts us to a zone of life that resists the governmentalizing and controlling forces of political life, but this zone of indeterminacy must lie in a continuous agonistic struggle with the exigencies imposed upon it by political life. The relationship between the personal and the impersonal must be read as a relationship between order, and conflict and resistance. The personal and the impersonal, then, cannot be split into two bifurcated realms, in which the latter is seen to overcome the former thereby causing a *lapsus* into a Hobbesian-like mythical origin that must be overcome. One wonders, however, whether the possibility of resistance that arises in the struggle between the personal and impersonal suffers from an excess of hope that ignores the real possibility that the very struggle between them may result in the obliteration of both, as human beings are now technologically capable of obliterating their own species. Moreover, one wonders whether the connection between biological and political life, as described within an immunitary framework, works in the way Esposito claims. Finally, given the claims above, the dynamism of the impersonal in the immunological paradigm defended by Esposito makes a genuine moment of impasse impossible as the tension between life and death constantly undoes the possibility of duration of a status quo, that is, the stasis of the conflict between life and death that would mark a possible impasse. The movement of life itself, its living, its virtuality, to borrow from Bergson and Deleuze, make impasse impossible.

Resistance in Immunity: Life, Person, and the Impersonal

For Esposito, life is not simply a generic concept; it needs to be highly individuated and it becomes this through embodiment or what he calls incorporation (IM 112–113). The meaning of corporeal or embodied life occupies a significant space in Esposito's work, which I cannot develop fully here, but I do wish to highlight the important constitutive elements of his view. Corporeal individuation establishes confines or borders, which act as a line of defense against whatever threatens to take life away from itself, and expel it to the outside, or reverse it into its opposite (IM 113). It is only in the body that life can remain what it is and even grow, reproduce, and be strengthened. Esposito describes the body as a privileged locus for the unfolding of life (IM 113). It is also the site where death becomes visible in the phenomena of aging, sickness, and physical deterioration. The goal of the body is to try and prevent as long as possible death and sickness; it struggles against its inevitable demise, and as such, becomes the "battleground" or "frontline" where the struggle between life and death occurs (IM 114). The body uses its own immunological process to defend itself, thereby creating the conditions that can guarantee its own survival. This is an autonomic process, and political interventions undertaken to control biological life, at least until now, have faced the risk of being undone by the body's own immunity system. Of course, this is not an absolute given, for the immune system also runs the risk of failing. Unlike Foucault, Esposito sees embodied biological life as possibly altering, resisting, or fighting political attempts to control and manipulate it.

A zone of indeterminacy or ambiguity exists within the core of the immunological paradigm: at the same time that an individuated corporeal being lives, it simultaneously dies. We all know that as we age, we die; we live while dying. The body's immune system works constantly to rid the organism of potential life-ending threats, and does so continuously until life ceases. The third person, the impersonal or the negative self, all equivalent terms, designates that originary space or zone situated in the body's own immune system in which the body kills threats and parts of itself in order to continue living. In this space, according to Esposito, the biological differentiation between living and dying is not quite firmly delineated (IM 151): one is not sure at what point something is living or dying.

If Esposito situates the negative self or impersonal within the immunological paradigm where an originary space arises between the living and dying of an organism, the self can be conceived neither in a substantive sense nor in identitarian terms. He writes, "Rather than a first person, that self has become a third person: not a 'he' or 'she,' but the nonperson who bears both its reality and its shadow." Esposito's third person is also described as the impersonal (TP 19–20). The impersonal is understood as a confluence, a crossing (*varco*) of various forces:

Rather than acting as a barrier for selecting and excluding elements from the outside world, [the immune dynamic] acts as a sounding board for the presence of the world inside the self. The self is no longer a genetic constant or a pre-established repertoire, but rather a construct determined by a set of dynamic factors, compatible groupings, fortuitous encounters; nor is it a subject or an object, but rather, a principle of action.... It is never original, complete, intact, 'made' once and for all; rather, it constantly makes itself from one minute to the next, depending on the situation and encounters that determine its development. Its boundaries do not lock it up inside a closed world; on the contrary, they create its margin, a delicate and problematic one to be sure, but still permeable in its relationship with that which, while still located outside it, from the beginning traverses it and alters it.

(IM 169)

The self is not conceived as a product of forces, but as the site of various dynamic forces and encounters that intersect.

Esposito's negative self certainly fits within a stream of nineteenth- and twentieth-century continental European philosophy, from Kierkegaard to Nietzsche, and Heidegger to Deleuze, that wishes to undo modern notions of the subject. His specific contribution to this debate can be seen in both his original political analysis and his view of selfhood localized in our immunity system. "From an immunological standpoint," he writes:

The "self" is defined only negatively, based on what it is not. This is the paradoxical conclusion, but one that is irrefutable, at least starting from the assumptions of the interpretative approach that passes from Ehrlich to the theory of clonal selection: as implicit in the evocative concept of *horror autotoxicus*, if the self recognized itself in an immune form, it would annihilate itself. The only way to survive is to be unaware of oneself. The object of the immune function, in short is never the self (except, of course, in the catastrophic case of autoimmune diseases) but rather everything that is not self. The "self" can only be immunologically expressed in the negative.

(IM 175)

At this point, we have to pause and ask where the force of Esposito's negation lies: Is the self simply a relation in which it always fails to identify with what it encounters by negating what is encountered? But Esposito rejects this view and maintains:

More than a simple logic of negation, it seems to refer to a contradiction by which identity is simultaneously affirmed and altered at the same time: it is established in the form of its own alteration. Like the pronoun that names it and the root from which the pronoun descends, the immunological self would thus be that which is more individual and that which is more shared. By overlaying these two divergent meanings onto one figure, what we get is the unique profile of a shared individuality or a sharing of individuality across bodies or across a collective body. It is perhaps in this chiasm that the enigma of immunity still lies preserved.

(IM 177)

The self that emerges from Esposito's analysis can be understood, in my view, to consist of two key elements. First, the self is not a construct but rather a crossing of different forces that arise within the operation of the immunological paradigm of life. Second, the self does have an identity, but that identity is spread across other individuals that form a plurality or community, much like function is dispersed across different cells in the medical paradigm. The notion of the self that is defined as being identical with itself, as being an analytical proposition, is displaced for an identity spread out over and in other individuals.

The negative self, or third person, must not only be read in isolation from the personal. If the logic of the immunitary paradigm is to be upheld, the conflict and resistance constitutive of life must extend to the struggle between the governmentalized person and the impersonal. In his recently published essay, *Le persone e le cose*,[45] Esposito claims that the person has undergone two extreme forms of governmentalization: it has been exclusively understood as possessor and/or property owner, as evidenced by the various legal definitions of the person as owner of property, from ancient Rome to the present; and it has undergone an abstraction through metaphysical thinking, especially in German Idealism and Phenomenology—its real, thingly nature, its embodiedness or very corporeity, has been evacuated (PC 24–28).

Esposito argues that the body, the living and lived body, though subject to more and more governmentalization by biotechnologies, still manages to resist the depersonalization of persons and the metaphysical abstraction that has happened to real things. In fact, the body, understood as a genuine site of resistance, can bring together persons and things, but it is also the locus that exceeds and cannot be completely subject to biopolitical governmentalization. The living body and even the "body politic" can resist governmentalization for various reasons. First, the body is a living entity in its own right and has built into itself the very immunological paradigm of birth, death, sickness, and resistance that Esposito attributes to all life. One never says, I am my body; rather, I have a body. Yet, the body is who we are (PC 89). "The reason that the body exceeds the great division between persons and things lies in the fact that it is neither ascribable to either things or persons" (PC 88).[46]

Second, the law generally has no status for the body: the law concentrates on persons, and persons do not always have bodies. Various legal entities, such as corporations, are persons, but they do not have a body.

> If law tends to erase the body, philosophy includes it within its very own horizon, but within a form of subordination. Without repeating a metaphysical Platonic gesture, nor turning our backs towards it, modern thought situates the body within the register of the object. The body is that which the subject recognizes, within itself but different than itself. In order to investigate the body, the subject must separate itself from it and keep the [object-body] at a distance. Here, Descartes's position is exemplary.
>
> (PC 80)[47]

Finally, the incorporation that a body assumes as a living being need not always result in a one—single individual; rather, incorporation can produce a multiplicity of bodies that transcend the individual. Nowhere is this clearer than when it comes to the relationship between the living body and technology:

> Naturally, the moving bridge that connects to technological objects is our very own body. Not only the mind, in which these objects

bear their symbolic and functional aspects but also the bodily signs deposited in them in the very act of their invention. The passing from one operator's hand to another creates a continual flow that moves beyond the singular individual to that "transindividual" dimension to which Simondon devoted his major work.

(PC 100)[48]

The possibility of transindividuation, which is part of the living body that exceeds the very limited notions of person and things given to us over the centuries by both philosophy and the law, becomes evident in something like the body politic. A multiplicity of bodies can unify in order to resist and combat any perceived threat. A multiplicity of bodies can unite to create something new and unexpected, for example, a new form of political organization or rule.

Something of the body politic remains external to its borders. When huge masses cram into the public squares of the world, as is happening today, we discover something that precedes their demands. Even before being pronounced, their words are incarnated in bodies that move in unison, with the same rhythm and in a unique emotive wave. Even though a locus of mobilization, without living bodies soldered together by the same energy, not even the web can become the new subject to come. Since first formulated in the event constitutive of the first modern democracy, the phrase 'we, the people' has a performative character; it produced the effect of creation in its very declaration. From that point forward, any linguistic act that sought to enter onto the political scene required a mouth and a throat, the breath of bodies next to one another in order to hear what the other says and to see what everyone else is doing.

(PC 110)[49]

A body can be both multiple and united; it can speak and declare. With its declarations it can make things happen, and define itself and the world around it. This is the power of the body politic, and this power can resist what comes to destroy it.

As Long as There Is Life, There Is Hope and the Possibility of Resistance?

Esposito is a philosopher of hope: he is very aware of growing governmentalization, instrumentalization, and the expansive force of biopolitical regimes, yet his very conception of life, in which one situates the personal, things, the impersonal, and resistance, as well as the conflict that unites them all, may contain (but not necessarily) the possibility of resistance to oppressive and destructive systems and disease that seek to destroy life itself. He locates his hope within the very structure of the living body that always seeks to incorporate itself in ways that transcend traditional forms of singularity and oneness ultimately moving toward the multiplicity of political bodies—transindividuated, living bodies. Certainly, the appeal to multiplicity echoes the idea of Antonio Negri's multitude. But does the hope of transindividuation and the impersonal not create other risks and challenges? In short, the answer is yes: Esposito conceives of biological life through the governmentalized eyes of Western Liberal democracy, and he does not consider the limits of such a view. Also, the fact that biology itself makes possible the very governmentality that seeks to control political life says something about the biology Esposito describes as immunological: perhaps biological life structures and moves political life towards governmentality, thereby causing us to rethink the relation between biological and political life.

The conflict and order that arise through the immunological paradigm that characterizes life carry with them certain assumptions. First, they assume that life operates and will perhaps continue to operate in the way Esposito understands it. But there is a precariousness to life, which Esposito acknowledges, especially in the discussion of risk that informs his work. The resistance on the part of life and the creativity it offers in terms of the living body and incorporation, as discussed above, is also assumed to be a possibility in Esposito's model. But, given the advances in bioengineering and the sciences in general, human beings have evolved to a stage where they can potentially destroy themselves as a species, either chemically, through atomic weapons, or through various viruses and diseases. This marks a new epoch in human evolution. We know of no other species that has consciously developed the means to destroy itself on such a mass scale. This possibility of self annihilation presents a challenge: though life may continue, human life may not. Moreover, there is no guarantee that the human species will come back from, resist, or even survive its own self-destruction. Esposito's thought is marked by a real distinction between biological life and political life: they stand to one another in a vis-à-vis relation. But, in fact, our own biology, our own development—body, brain, and mind—has helped produce and condition the very possibility of our destruction. This raises the question: Has our own biology given rise to the governmentalization that has resulted in the possibility of our obliteration as both a biological and political species? Perhaps the Aristotelian difference between biological and political life is not so stark; perhaps our own biology has facilitated the very governmentalization that seeks to control and even destroy us. Furthermore, the real possibility of our annihilation as a species poses a challenge to Esposito's notion of the body politic, for we can destroy biological human life and political life as we know it: this means resistance and hope may be finite. It also means that life itself, as it evolves, bringing about order and conflict, may create the very conditions for its own demise, its own end.

But the move from biological life to political life is too quick, too slippery: Esposito has assumed that politics, following Aristotle, is a form of life, a *bíos*. I question whether the immunological structure of biological life necessarily reproduces itself in the body politic in the way Esposito indicates. One certainly sees the immunological paradigm play itself out in dominant Liberal models of Western democracy, but politics comes in numerous forms, even in forms that resist the immunological paradigm. All around the globe political forms of life exist that need not work through a dialectic of order, conflict, resistance, risk, life, and death. For example, various forms of anarchism or intentional communities, in which consensus, discussion, and mutual collaboration abound, can be seen as resisting Esposito's own immunological depiction of life. Also, various Buddhist communities around the world view life not in immunological terms, but as a cycle of flow in which we participate and share.

It would be absurd to claim there is absolutely no relationship between biological life and political life, as the way we organize ourselves is dependent upon meeting certain basic biological needs, which political life can facilitate and expedite, or even destroy. But to claim that the immunological view of biological life defines life presents a huge problem, as this view is largely seen from the perspective of the evolution and devolution of Liberal democracy. Political life need not exclusively configure itself in the immunological way Esposito describes, even though biological life may operate in the immunological manner he describes.

Granted, Esposito painstakingly details how the biological view of life has been transformed into the immunological paradigm through shifts in medicine and politics, and though this may be true for Western Liberal democracies, one wonders whether this is a limited view; the rich, multifaceted reality of biological life is not easily confinable to philosophical definitions, a point Esposito himself makes throughout his work. What would Esposito make of the differing views of biological life found in other traditions, for example, those found in Chinese medicine or within various Indigenous healing practices? Different biological models of life exist, and though immunity is an important aspect, it is not necessarily the central defining principle. More than a critique of Esposito, the aforementioned comments can be read perhaps as confirming the power of life to reconfigure itself in different forms, biologically and politically. Moreover, the connection between biological life and the political life or the body politic might not be as direct or strict as Esposito tells us, especially outside of dominant Western paradigms of Liberal politics.

What are the implications of these critiques for political hope and resistance? As we saw earlier, hope for the new, for change, for the dissipation of destructive and violent forms of politics, and for the birth of a new political order is rooted in the immunological paradigm, specifically in the resistance of life to governmentalization. Though such hope is possible, it is not necessary. Moreover, this hope is fragile: it may never come to be, given the real possibility of life destroying itself: the annihilation of the human species by the human species. But any form of real hope is not simply a matter of probabilities, even biological ones. As Ernst Bloch, Gabriel Marcel, and others have pointed out, hope is an extreme form of anticipation in which something may come from a seeming nothingness. Hope is a genuine becoming, a newness that is not regulated by a structure of cause and effect, even the cause and effect of the immunological paradigm offered by Esposito.

Though there are limits to the hope that Esposito places in the life of the immunitary paradigm, some possibility of hope still exists. In the end, the resistance of biological life that conditions the possibility of resistance in the body politic offers us two forms of hope, one explicit and one implicit. Explicitly, if we accept the connection Esposito establishes between biological and political life in his immunitary paradigm, there is hope that the limits of governmentality and the impossibility of completely controlling biological life—which open up space, for example, for the interaction of forces that create the impersonal, the negative self, or even the impolitical—will allow life to incorporate itself, especially in transindividual, multiplex forms, and ultimately announce resistant new possibilities. A second, implicit form of hope lies within Leibniz's great question: Why is there something rather than nothing? In terms of Esposito's thought, and following Bergson, we can ask: Why is there life in the first place as opposed to nothing? That life exists at all, when it need not, is a real something that is not a nothing. Life is a newness that continues to become, and insofar as there is always life, human and nonhuman, this can be read as hope. Life is a chance becoming that continues, in the moment, to be, creating itself and bringing into being new moments of itself: life is the creative evolution that Bergson describes. Insofar as life itself offers the possibility of new becoming, it can possibly give hope of becoming otherwise both for biological life and political life.

Esposito's focus on living that is pushed along by the tension between life and death in the immunological paradigm creates possibilities, especially for resisting governmentalizing controls that seek to control biopolitical life. But as long as life continues to unfold, there is always an outside to any political system, an outside which is also contained in the very interiority of life itself, as seen above. Impasse, understood as a stasis, an in-between state in which no determination of power relations between the ruler and the ruled is forthcoming or possible, is antithetical to Esposito's system. If anything, certain biopolitical regimes may wish to create the illusion of impasse to bolster and sustain their own control, but this is a *fictio*, for they try to stave off the awareness of the very becoming of life and its potentials, both life-giving and noxious. In the end, the tension between conflict and order, which Esposito from his very first works on Machiavelli sees as central to politics and resistance, is inscribed in a robust conception of living that by definition will advance and move forward as far as it can. Life itself is in between life and death, but there is never a stasis. While this may be true biologically, it may not be the case at the level of political life or *zoe*, to borrow the Aristotelian conception of the *zoon politikon*. There are moments in political life when we find ourselves at an impasse. Many of us living in the contemporary world are neither rulers nor ruled. We are simply held in a state of suspended animation. What to do?

Possibility in the New Political Impasse

The new form of political impasse that we live marks a particular kind of power relation, not of the ruler over the ruled, but somewhere in between rulers and the ruled. But political impasses continue to offer thinking unique occasions, among other things, to imagine effective solutions and create new realities. Impasse may even provide the space and time, albeit sometimes very painful and violent, to think and bring about a new form of change, especially one from within ourselves. As we have seen from our investigation of Foucault, impasse, at best, may be seen as part of the being *en route* to resistance of a dominant power. But what do we do when we are stuck in this moment of impasse or when it perdures?

Furthermore, if we accept Foucault's minimum possibility of impasse, it would have to be inscribed within the logics of action upon action or subjectivation. But this action would have to be inscribed within the dynamic of the relations of force. Impasse itself, however, can exert a pressure on us, and the only place to turn is within: it creates the possibility of an auto-affective turn in which a realm of interiority may be cultivated. Foucault's later writings on the care of the self may be read as corrective or as a recognition of a broader understanding of action that makes way for intimate, personal understandings of subjectivity, but the therapeutic philosophical possibilities Foucault uncovers in his analysis of ancient Greek and Roman thinkers must still be inscribed within his lifelong commitment to uncovering modes of resistance to dominant powers, even within the framework of his discussion of self-care. Impasse is not part of the Foucaultian conception of the self.

Impasse can become a time of thought, imagination, and political debate and discourse. And though the ideas may be ineffective against the force of the impasse itself, what is important to preserve is not so much viability of the pragmatic outcome of the ideas or the ultimate power to bring about some change, but the capacity to give birth to such ideas and imaginings. It is this potential that can still remain active in impasse, but we must not make this potential exclusively dependent on the success or concretion or realization of the outcomes of the thinking and the imagination. Impasse can be a realm in which one may cultivate the sheer potentiality of thinking and the imagination to conceive reality otherwise. Both can and must be kept alive. This is one, but not the exclusive, condition that can help bring about political change aimed at human collective flourishing.

The Ancients have insights to offer on impasse. Plato makes much of impasse, especially in his early dialogues. He calls them *aporia*, literally, gaps that cannot be crossed. Socrates sometimes describes impasse as a paralysis, both of body and mind. At other times, *aporia* calls for questioning and investigation. Plato recounts, for example, the story of Socrates stopping Euthyphro to question him about his presence at the courthouse.[50] Euthyphro tells Socrates he is prosecuting his father for killing a worker who murdered a slave, and that this prosecution is on religious grounds: he is being pious by following what the gods command, namely, justice for the death of an innocent person. Socrates begins to question Euthyphro on the meanings of piety and impiety. In the end, all of Euthyphro's efforts to define piety and impiety fail. Rather than continue to pursue the debate, he tells Socrates that he must run off to complete a certain task as he is late. The dialogue ends with an impasse: we do not know what piety or impiety really is, and Socrates does not offer a solution to this dilemma.

Whether it is a discussion on the nature of virtue, language, the good, pleasure, or even love, Socrates often leads his readers, sometimes frustratingly so, to an *aporia*. But *aporia* for Socrates is not without purpose. Hannah Arendt reminds us that Socratic *aporia* leads us to think, and to think over and over again about what we say and what we do. For Arendt, it is Socrates who embodies the epitome of what it means to think. He is gripped by wonder—he does not *need* to wonder—and it pushes him to ask questions, to dialogue with himself and others, to try to answer the unanswerable. In this sense, Socrates also seeks meaning, but his search, at least as Plato depicts it in the early dialogues, ends in *aporia*: there is a genuine impasse.

The three crucial aspects of thinking for Socrates—the sting and its paralysis, the moral function, and the maieutic role—are discussed in metaphorical terms by Arendt.[51] One of the more important things that thinking does is stop us in our tracks. When we think, we pause to ponder what is manifest before us. Arendt describes many situations in which Socrates is paralyzed by thought, as if he has been temporarily stunned by a stingray, and this paralysis interrupts his life. He stops and begins to wonder, to give thanks to the gods or make reparation for some kind of omission. Recall the beginning of the *Phaedrus*, in which Socrates is suddenly gripped by the thought that he has somehow offended the gods just as he is set to engage in discussions about the nature of love.

Arendt, invoking Socrates, also notes that thought, like a gadfly, stings. Socrates engages various elite members of Athenian society, usually asking them to clarify what they mean when they describe their thoughts or deeds. Inevitably, neither Socrates nor his interlocutor can fully answer the question on which the dialogue centers. Euthyphro, for example, knows he must fulfill some ritual obligation, but neither he nor Socrates knows what piety is. Socrates stings his interlocutors—he is the gadfly that annoys his dialogue partners because he shows them they know nothing, or at least not what they thought they knew with such conviction. In this way, he urges them to think more consciously about what they are doing, both as individuals and as members of society.

Arendt points out that thinking, for Socrates, is not only connected with this paralyzing and stinging function but also gives birth to ideas. It is maieutic. The role of the ancient Greek midwife was to help with the birth of a child, but also to decide whether the child was fit to live or die. Socrates, as midwife, helps bring ideas, that is, thought-things, to presence. In his dialogues, he deliberates whether the things brought forward in thought should live or die; this is the nature of the *elenchus*. In dialectical thinking, one can examine and critique various thoughts and their implications and/or omissions. Desire does not enter into Arendt's discussion of Socratic thinking.

Both Socrates and Arendt understand thinking to have a moral function. While thought can stop us in our tracks so we pause to wonder at what is manifest before us, while it can give birth to new ideas and things, it also allows us to ponder and judge what we have before us. Thinking makes things appear, but judging helps us distinguish between what is good and bad, beautiful and ugly. Arendt remarks:

> I shall show that my own main assumption in singling out judgment as a distinct capacity of our minds has been that judgments are not arrived at by either deduction or induction; in short, they have nothing in common with logical operations.... We shall be in search of the "silent sense," which—when it was dealt with at all—has always, even in Kant, been thought of as "taste" and therefore as belonging to the realm of aesthetics.[52]

It is thinking, according to Arendt, that allows Socrates to put forward two important ethical dicta: "It is better to be wronged than do wrong," and "It would be better for me that my lyre or a chorus I directed should be out of tune and loud with discord and that multitudes of men should disagree with me rather than I, being one, should be out of harmony with myself and contradict me."[53] The banality of evil that Arendt attributed to Adolf Eichmann, for example, was an issue of his thoughtlessness; the destruction and violence of his crimes might have been avoided if he had stopped to think and had taken responsibility for what thought brought forward.

But the notion of impasse I wish to address is not only that of an impasse in thinking to reach any new insights or possibilities. Individuals who find themselves in the new political impasse find themselves somewhere in between the more direct and classical relationship of power we have called the ruler–ruled. Aporetic impasses, as described above, can happen within the frameworks of ruler–ruled. Indeed, Socrates belonged to the elite ruling class of Athens: he was a citizen. It should be remarked here that though we often find the term "political impasse" deployed in works of political theory and political science—to refer to a stalemate, a cul-de-sac, some sort of blockage—we do not have a theory of this kind of impasse.

Bill Martin's *Politics in the Impasse: Explorations in Post-Secular Theory* makes the claim that impasse is to be understood in both historical and political terms as the failure to overcome hegemony; impasse is a kind of exhaustion (of the Left).[54] Martin calls for a radical form of community to break the impasse, a community that is genuinely pluralist and free of racism and sexism. He views impasse as a state of powerlessness (read being ruled by an oppressive, ruling force) that is inscribed in a broader framework of oppression. When speaking of the various impasses of the European Union, Donald Kalff describes them as a "lack" of ideas to think Europe's future and as "yielding nothing."[55] There are numerous articles that discuss political impasses in various countries, but, in these cases, impasse means that legislation cannot go forward or that the parties involved in a certain situation cannot come to some meaningful resolution or agreement.[56]

If we accept my claim about the existence of a group of people that experiences a new political impasse, it seems that I have confined such a phenomenon to our present age. But if we explore the margins of philosophy, the other side of the canon, we find philosophers who have articulated and experienced the sense of political impasse I have described. And what they offer us is valuable for rethinking impasse as a political phenomenon.

The notion of political impasse is not new to political philosophy. In fact, Neo-Stoic thinkers like Guilaume du Vair and Justus Lipsius meditate on its profound nature. In his elegantly written and thoughtful essay *On Constancy*,[57] Lipsius, in the home of one of his old friends, admits after much questioning that there are genuine situations in which one's ability to bring about any real, significant political change is limited by conflict between entrenched factions that are unwilling to cede any recognition and validity to the opposing side; positions are so firm that the only alternative possible is an enforced one. Lipsius, of course, is referring to the war of religions, which his beloved Flanders was then enduring. He recounts his subjection to the negative effects of war and religious persecution. Being subjected to a given politics with no possibility of changing it or curtailing its brutal excesses is paramount to understanding the phenomenon of political impasse. One's subjectivity and agency is deeply restricted by the powers that be. One submits, or one faces the peril of destruction.

Fortunately, Lipsius has the means and the connections to flee to safe harbor in Germany. He admits that the civil wars raging in his native land cause him both physical and mental injury. It is important to note here that Lipsius, though suffering, still has the freedom to move and escape the full effects of the war. In this sense, he might be seen as one who is neither completely oppressed nor capable of making any real change. Lipsius draws upon both Stoic philosophy and Christian theology to find some kind of healing. Physically, he chooses to move outside the zone of conflict, but the trauma lingers and afflicts his soul. The philosopher admits that fleeing alone is not sufficient to deal with the deeply negative effects of violence and political impasse. Neither can he lose himself in fantasies of the imagination, which only defer the reality of the situation.

Lipsius's response is to unpack what it is to live in a time of political impasse. He invokes the Stoic notion of fate, always interwoven with a thick notion of Christian providence, to describe his situation. Fate is to be understood as a kind of necessity in which one's own freedom is severely limited. One must learn to accept and respond to what is given as there is no viable alternative. Lipsius calls upon the notion of constancy (*constantia*, a difficult term to translate into English) as key to bearing impasse: it is a virtue that connotes strength, perseverance, and discipline of mind.

Constancy is sustainable for Lipsius because of his own theological view of God. He subscribes to traditional theodicy in which, seen from God's view of the eternal present, what may seem tragic to humans in any given moment may be only a certain stage of development that aims at the eventual realization of ultimate perfection and goodness. Reminiscent of Boethius's classical argument concerning the providence of God, Lipsius's own belief conditions the very possibility of constancy in the first place. But what if one does not believe in Lipsius's Christian God? What can one do in such times of impasse?

Lipsius gives a very traditional Stoic answer here: thicken one's understanding of oneself, thereby empowering the self to develop attitudes and resources that will help ease the pain and suffering. This self is a source of free thinking, and thought itself can bring relief, but it also helps distinguish practicable alternatives. The turn inward, into a zone of selfhood that can resist or even remain unaffected by political impasse, is vital. I take inspiration from Lipsius's approach, but I also think we need to develop it to tackle the noxious effects of political impasse.

But how can political impasse produce a kind of thinking otherwise, an opening to change and being otherwise? Have we not just returned to the Platonic *aporia*? One arrives at *aporia*, for Plato, through dialectical thinking: one questions and answers, collects and divides, and examines thoughts to better understand the nature of something. Platonic impasses of thought push one to think again and deeper, to think anew. Political impasse, as I describe it, builds on the Platonic urgency to think anew, but the impetus to think does not stem from an internal need or eros; rather, the external situation of political impasse imposes itself upon us and affects us. It can stymie any action or thought, it can simply render us "stuck" or immobile without any hope of a genuine response—we are forced to stand by—or it can push us to think otherwise. But to think otherwise a certain sense of self must merge with or manifest itself through the very pressure caused by the impasse. This pressure causes an auto-affection: we undergo the impasse and a self that is confined begins to emerge, a self that longs for an end to the impasse and seeks some solution to it. Thinking in political impasse is, then, an affect elicited by the situation's constraints. The affect of constraint reveals a self that *feels itself* constrained and desires *a way out as well as its own freedom.*

3

Impasse and the Recovery and Transformation of Selfhood

Recovery of a Zone of Selfhood That Is *Our* Own: *Oikeiosis*

The Ancients believed that all human beings, including children, naturally seek to become and be at home *in themselves* through a process of self-appropriation (*oikeiosis*). Making ourselves at home, being fully at home in ourselves, is a form of self-creation, and the most fundamental way we exist in the world. But this possibility is stymied by the new impasse. A long list of modern thinkers has systematically shown how the relation of the ruler–ruled structures subjectivity and selfhood, both positively and negatively. Think of Nietzsche's debtor–creditor relationship, for example, or Hegel's master–slave dialectic. Because we are fully neither ruler nor ruled, any complete subjectivation, especially oikeiotic self-becoming, is blocked. We live this blockage in impasse.

Making the self a home, or becoming at home in oneself, is not a being-there (*Da-sein*) as Heidegger describes it in his monumental work *Being and Time*. Heidegger's description of the thrownness of our being is postulated on what he sees as an existential fact: we do not choose to exist. His notion of the human being begins with self-alienation. On the contrary, the Roman poet Lucretius, in his *De rerum natura*, claims one sees even in the infant, in its interactions with its parents, a desire to be at home with itself and the world. In fact, both Lucretius and Cicero see this desire in all of nature; part of the development of living creatures involves this sense of being at home and finding one's place. A sense of ownness, which need not be grasped as an experience of self-identity (that is, selfhood as an identity of the self-same), typifies the modern I or ego—one knows that one is at home with oneself not only because nature orders us to be this way but also because we feel it and desire it to be so. Our very survival depends on it. This relationship with the world, others, and ourselves is conceived by the Ancients as being harmonious and synchronized; only when we live, as Epictetus instructs, according to nature, according to what fate has given us. *Oikeiosis* happens before our very own consciousness of it or prior to our own understanding of our wills and minds. It should be remarked, however, that Lucretius's idea of *oikeiosis* is not exclusively postulated on the possibility of a subject's autonomy, as it is for Modern thinkers. The being at home with oneself of the Ancients is more about finding a place within one's own being, a residence of sorts wherein one can lodge, where one can linger and abide with oneself and, ultimately, become, as opposed to the Modern project of establishing a center of control, authority, self-ownership. The Ancients posit a different relationship to oneself, not an ego pole of identity, but a place where one can rest and be comfortable with oneself, where one need not be disturbed by overextended and exaggerated, and, therefore, painfully unachievable, projects of the colonizing desires of control, domination, and self-possession. In *oikeiosis*, we come to relate to ourselves differently than what the modern Western tradition of philosophy says we do.

Political impasse interrupts this natural desire and striving to be at home with oneself and others in the world, for the traditional defining poles of ruler–ruled are unable to structure themselves as they have in the past. In impasse we no longer feel at one with what is given and what we create; impasse stymies *oikeiosis*. Renaissance and Modern thinkers, including Justus Lipsius, tell us that a predicament of fate induced by political impasse limits freedom, whereas the Ancients convey that it frustrates a natural desire or even a natural structure—the fundamental integrity of nature—of which we are a part. Both the Ancients and the Moderns are right here, as a naturally occurring desire to belong and make the self one's own, as well as one's own determining agency are frustrated by political impasse; both of these phenomena contribute to the despair, helplessness, and the sense of abandon typical of impasse. But we also find ourselves waiting, waiting for change or, at least, a break that can produce change.

The Ancient Greek notion of *politeia*, among its many meanings, included as one of its constitutive aspects a kind of civic respect, or what Aristotle called *philia*. We learn in his *Nicomachean Ethics* that Aristotle believes *philia*—neighborly or brotherly love—is more important than justice for the flourishing of the polis; we need to cultivate *philia* to live well with one another. Abandonment, helplessness, and despair, the affects of impasse, not only block the desire to love, but also unhinge the social links that make such love possible. One is condemned to oneself as the desire to be social comes undone; the becoming of the self, understood as a kind of self-possession within a social world is blocked.

In addition to abandon and despair, the deep, fundamental affective structure of political impasse is marked by a profound sense of futility: no matter what we do, how we think, or how we act, nothing changes. We are stuck. But human beings are agents born to act; life is action and movement, and as Thomas Aquinas and Aristotle rightly claim, an action needs to be taken, enacted, to be considered truly fulfilled. Our frustration in political impasse extends primarily from this sense of futility. Still, not all senses of futility are the same; futility can arise from oppression and violence, from boredom and wealth, or from indifference. That a genuine sense of futility may arise from conditions in which certain factions of a society or an established order control and dominate other factions, especially through violence, exclusion, and subjugation, is an obvious claim to make. Protracted periods of war hang as heavy clouds upon the spirits of human beings and incite a cruel passivity and fatalism, especially civil wars that also obstruct a nation's own flourishing. Countless examples haunt human history.

The well-known account of the master–slave dialectic can only take place when clear lines of ruler and subject emerge, but when there is no clear winner and no clear loser, no defined lord and bondsman, political impasse takes hold and the relations between parties become a dolorous in-between state. If we examine the sense of futility that emerges, we see it is caused by: despair from the dashed hope of a swift, sure victory over the enemy; a frustrated desire to control what Augustine calls the *libido dominandi*; a lack of recognition from within and without of any clear winner or loser; and drained material resources causing physical and mental hardship. Curious in such states is the loss of a sense of the struggle's ultimate purpose and a sense of the self and its place in relation to others and the world. We must be clear: these futile states of impasse are not all-encompassing, as impasse is sometimes induced to profit certain parties, in which case the situation is still defined by the logic of the ruler–ruled: stronger parties will for weaker parties to be in a state of impasse. For example, in many contemporary conflicts, whether in Africa or the Middle East, arms dealers and the governments that sell arms have vested interests in keeping states and/or peoples in prolonged conditions of impasse. Also, these states can resolve or put on hold other potential problems as they can cause a distraction for certain factions which, if not occupied with one another, may turn and cause grief for other countries or parties. In other words, all states of impasse are not only that for everyone—there will always be those individuals or groups who stand to benefit.

Unlike the *ressentiment* and despair of the ruled, and unlike the force, dependency, and blindness of the ruler, the new impasse produces in its sufferers a true ambiguity, a real either–or, in which both the perspectives of the ruler and those of the ruled are seemingly viable and correct. Those living with impasse feel they can do nothing to change the fate of the binary of ruler–ruled, but they do not feel themselves completely burdened or seized by the ruler–ruled concept or enforcement of political power. In other words, the ambivalence is lived as an experience in which two seemingly opposite poles exist, with no possibility of either becoming ruler or ruled: on one hand, all possibilities for power exist at once; on the other hand, and simultaneously so, no possibilities exist at all. Everything seems possible, but nothing can be done. This is the true ambivalence of the new political impasse that affects millions of people worldwide. It cuts across class, ethnic divides, race, religion, sex, and gender.

Political impasse arises from the success of a desired or achieved *status quo* that lies between the ruler and the ruled. Here, one can call to mind most Western Liberal societies that have a comparatively high standard of living. I think, in particular, of countries like Canada, for example. A vast Canadian geography combined with a relatively contained population and economic prosperity has produced, for the most part, citizens who have very little to complain about *vis-à-vis* other developed countries. Voter turnout for municipal, provincial, and national elections is relatively low. Some corruption of political leaders at all levels of government is present, and those who do vote wait patiently for the next election's changeover. Most young Canadians, however, have little faith in their political leaders and choose not to vote or participate in politics. There are few mass manifestations demanding accountability and transparency over the use of public funds, and Canadians passively accept massive changes in financial policy, environmental control, and education. It would be naïve to think that this is simply a matter of "despite it all, things work." Etienne de la Boétie observes that people choose to follow; he calls this voluntary servitude. They are content with little and, as long as they have their *bonne soupe* at night, do not care about affairs of state.

This incredible, never previously experienced wealth and the somewhat successful distribution of it, which is now being limited in severe ways, can produce an impasse. How? Through business and the economy. Contemporary politics has become the privy of business and financial capitalists. The promise of easy money to obtain what most people cannot afford creates a social illusion of comfort, especially for the impassed living in Canada, for example. Large amounts of money are obtained, predicated on the payback over time, ultimately producing what Lazzarato calls the "indebted man."[1] This debt model of wealth creation has produced a society in which material needs and a desire to possess and own, what Augustine called the *libido habendi*, are fulfilled. Politics has been reduced to access to financial capital. Greater access to this capital has produced a society that is not only narrow-minded, but greedy, which in turn has created an unprecedented boredom with the self, the world, and others.

It has also produced a kind of political lethargy. The political promise of financial capital has been fulfilled, at least temporarily, but when the debt is no longer sustainable and the capital, our purchasing power, dries up, Canadians will become restless again. The imaginary created by financial wealth cannot be maintained, especially as it is predicated on larger economies propping it up, economies over which Canada has very little influence. The impasse caused by the unjust distribution of wealth arises in the complicit relation between consumer and financial capitalist. Each party has to work hard to keep the system afloat, otherwise everything will collapse and all of us will lose that which we have bought into; we have no real alternative other than boom and collapse. Furthermore, the fact that there is one encompassing system produces boredom since the need for novelty that stems from nineteenth-century industrialization, as Adorno observes, is restricted by a system that continues to reproduce itself in the same way everywhere, seducing people with empty promises of wealth and prosperity that are based simply on trust, time, and compliance with the aims of this new business system of financial capital. In Canada, a vast segment of the population is neither oppressed nor ruling. This does not mean, however, that the classic division of ruler–ruled does not exist, for an elite class of rulers certainly does exist and, sadly, there are many who find themselves at the margins of Canadian society, wrecked by poverty, inequity, racism, sexism, homophobia, transphobia, unemployment, illness, injustice, and violence.

Indifference can also produce a sense of futility. Though it can emerge from boredom, as discussed above, there is a species of indifference that results from a consuming preoccupation with one's own private world and one's own property, both intellectual and material. Technology concomitant with wealth has given us a more robust sense of ownness. The Liberal self has truly been achieved in our lifetime, sometimes with good consequences as we enjoy greater self-autonomy, but also with deleterious effects, as we have become indifferent to those that exist outside what we have defined as our own "sphere of ownness," what Husserl and Edith Stein call the *Eigenheitssphäre*. Ideally, we wish to be with others, yet we prefer that the others make no demands on us, especially ethical or material ones. It is as if all that which is peripheral to our own sense of self is unimportant or simply marginal. Yet, what lies in the periphery is vital. We have turned away from the world—a world Arendt tried to save with her own view of politics— and, with this turn, we have closed off the possibility of politics and genuine change. In our Liberal atomization, we have cut ourselves off from the larger social reality which has been, traditionally, the object of politics. The distinction between our own subjectivity and the world is collapsed and only our own subjectivity stands, a super subjectivity composed of very distinct private spheres that interact out of necessity rather than out of a genuine desire to build a political community, not of selves, but of a collectivity of those who share in a common life. This impoverished sense of the self and its seclusion from others and the world frustrates the natural process of *oikeiosis*—a process that sees being at home as deeply social.

But if we closely examine our sphere of ownness, we find that the subjectivity promised by modern philosophy and politics is absent, as it has been thoroughly determined and shaped by the massive forces of social and political organization that have evolved over the last twenty years. The public discourse and ideology that dominate Western Liberal political life revolve around rights and freedoms and personal choice, but the reality on the ground is quite different: we find a fairly homogeneous group of privileged individuals who enjoy a level of economic comfort, as well as a large number of people who may have enough money to survive but cannot live like the privileged few. Despite this inequality, the system persists—a system that continues to generate inequality, but which we are powerless to organize against or bring down. The modern promise of equality is still spoken, and most of us subscribe to this promise in one form or another, but it is far from delivered. For many, this is still an empty promise.

The project of the modern self, which we can term here self-becoming, and which is part of the traditional understanding of *oikeiosis*, has been deemed too expensive and inefficient. To continue with our Canadian example, the self of the classical Liberal model of education has been displaced. Our education system has radically changed over the last two decades: the disciplines that encourage and cultivate true and free self-becoming have been relegated to service courses—such as philosophy for engineering students, offered at basic levels and in limited amounts—or worse, entirely eliminated. Fields of study such as literature, philosophy, history, foreign languages, music, and art—all potentially creative harbors that give refuge to the soul as it finds the time and space to create new possibilities—face certain extinction in institutions of higher learning as they are deemed self-indulgent, unproductive, or irrelevant. Humanities programs are dying everywhere as they cannot deliver a job, another promise of the new business politics. Nearly half of most students registered in North American universities and colleges are in some form of business program. It is economically impossible for markets to absorb the number of students in such programs; therefore, marketized universities cannot fulfill the promises they make. This is why business programs have moved from managerial models of instruction to innovation and creativity models: every student is to generate or "create" a self-subsistent economy. Responsibility for the economy, usually understood as a collective effort, has been downloaded onto the shoulders of individual creators. Yet, the social capital that drives the economy in general continues to be drawn upon but, in a schizoid fashion, ignored or downplayed. Most students have been influenced by this kind of instruction and come to university with no desire for self-becoming; they simply wish to have a job and university is to provide them with some kind of training which, for the most part, it does not do.

The Emergence of World, the Inner, and Auto-Affection

Interiority and the recovery of a zone of selfhood that is made possible through the pressure of impasse do not mean we are trapped in our immanence. Within auto-affection comes the oikeiotic possibility of a world filled with relations. A world comes to exist and continues to persist primarily through its affect, which is disclosed in the intimacy of what Michel Henry and other phenomenologists call auto-affection. The disclosure of world, like the manifestation of the self, is revealed in a primary experience of auto-affection; the revelation persists because of its primary impression upon us through the sensations, feelings, and meanings it elicits in us. Our continued response to these impressions which are grasped even before we are fully conscious of them, and which the world affects in us, allows the world to persist and unfold in time, a world that is not only inner but also external, that is transcendent, to use Husserlian language.

The worlding of the inner oikeiotic turn must not simply be read as the controversial idea of inner emigration developed by writers like Frank Thieß.[2] Though writers and philosophers have developed the idea in a variety of senses, one of the enduring criticisms of inner emigration is that it was a willful decision to turn inward and disconnect from the deadly and disastrous political situation of the Third Reich in Germany to seek solace and safety in an interior life, abandoning the demand for responsibility and active resistance and action.[3] Less critical views see the inner turn as not only providing safety, but also as making possible a form of resistance and even creative artistic possibilities.[4] The oikeiotic possibility that impasse announces allows for a rethinking of oneself, others, and world, ultimately and hopefully yielding new possibilities of social and political life. Oikeiosis can restructure our relationships to ourselves that may possibly create new understandings of ourselves, others, and the world, ultimately creating the possibility of a new understanding of politics and sociality.

The Manifestation of a World from Within

Part of being at home includes the feeling that one lives and has a world in which one belongs. Hannah Arendt in the *Origins of Totalitarianism* observes that one of the ways that totalitarian states prepared the way for the murder of millions of Jews and others was to ensure that the stateless not only lacked legal recognition of citizenship but also a sense of home.[5] She notes that totalitarian regimes rise, in part, as a response to impasse, though she does not pause to reflect on the quality or nature of impasse itself.[6] A world that frames the sense of what it is to be at home with oneself never begins purely as a willed project; it is only grasped secondarily, in a retrospective apprehension or experience. Often, by the time we are conscious of a world, it has already and largely been shaped. While it is true that one can conceive of a new world, in the best sense of utopian thinking, the world is experienced in part as a projection, but the desire, sentiments, and past experiences that help build that imaginary image of a new world have already been laid in the pre-conscious sediments of passive synthesis. It may also be said that we build our worlds as if only our conscious desires, experiences, acts, and relations participate in the process. It would be absurd to deny the force of this conscious world building, but the world also consists of sedimented layers of meaning or sense derived from the passive experience of sensations, drives, desires, habits, and unconscious motivations. A world contains, for example, all kinds of unconscious sensibilities and attitudes that have been built over time and that may only manifest themselves consciously at certain moments of waking experience. It would seem that the possibility of a world, understood as a series of coherences of sense, to borrow an expression from the phenomenologist Edith Stein,[7] has both active and passive elements that help it emerge and take shape.

Michel Henry argues that the traditional phenomenological approach to understanding sense building, which includes both transcendental and genetic analysis, is rooted in an intentional logic of noesis and noema, that is, phenomenology focuses on the intentional acts and objects of consciousness.[8] He maintains that what phenomenology generally never accounts for is the possibility of manifestation itself. Manifestation or appearing is simply assumed to be a given of reality, but there is no account of how appearing happens in the first place.[9] Henry puts forward the idea that a primary receptivity lodged at the core of the possibility of experience itself makes possible an auto-affection that permits appearing to appear; that is, auto-affection, understood as the very awareness of the self, is the condition for the possibility of any appearing (EM 227–230). The self is revealed as an embodied I, subject to time and capable of sensation, will, and reason, that is ultimately constituted as a person in Henry's later works.[10] But auto-affection is not only an originary site in which appearing first comes to manifest itself; it is also a site where life reveals itself, a life that is prior to any kind of determination, a life we do not control and that sustains us. For most phenomenologists, the world is a coherence of sense or a referential totality that is built up from the conscious and passive content of experience; the world is not coeval with the primary site of appearing, auto-affection, and living. I would like to reverse this claim: the world is primarily disclosed and must be understood as a fundamental placing or embeddedness in a coherent whole of sense, which allows the primary sensations (*Empfindnisse*) constitutive of experience itself, namely, appearing, self, and life, to be positioned *vis-à-vis* and related to one another and the eventual layers of content, both static and genetic, constitutive of wider frameworks of experience and meaning.

Husserl's insistence on intentionality being the foundational structure of consciousness assumes that the fullness or achievement of appearing, which gives material content to both noesis and noema, coincides with the adequation of noeses and noemata themselves. Manifestation makes things appear and then consciousness works on what is given. Noesis and noema belong to a reduced sphere of consciousness, which is arrived at through eidetic variation and the willed taking on of a phenomenological stance.[11] If one closely reads Husserl's intentional analyses, noesis and noema organize and give sense to what comes to present or manifest itself in consciousness. Yet, for Michel Henry, appearing does not necessarily coincide with noeses and noemata: it is a much more foundational phenomenon that is not dependent on the constitutional analyses of Husserlian phenomenological consciousness. How then does appearing appear?, asks Michel Henry.

Appearing can be understood as a fundamental givenness over which we have no control. Appearing affects us: it elicits our passive receptive sensibility, awakening in us its manifesting force. In a very deep way, we are overcome, subject, and receptive to appearing, and, for Henry, the disclosure of manifestation happens at a passive level through our capacity to be affected by the sensations of appearing. Affectivity is that which makes the appearance of things appear (EM 240–249). Angela Ales Bello, reading Husserl's lectures on passive synthesis and Edith Stein's *Philosophy of Psychology*, remarks that noetic is dragged behind (PPH 158–159) the hyletic or passive structures of consciousness. Passive sensations or sense-impressions make us aware that there is an appearing that has not yet constituted itself as an intentional object.[12] The warmth of the sun on our faces, the pain of the bitter cold, the pleasure of our successes, the shade of red on the rose, the pleasure of color—these are all examples of sensations we experience that are constituted as classical intentional objects of consciousness. Coeval with such sensations is a primary form of appearing, namely, affectivity.

Our very affectivity allows manifestation to show itself as it impresses itself upon us. Henry argues that the primacy of affectivity makes two foundational realities that are co-given with manifestation itself appear simultaneously: the self and life.[13] Affective experience begins at the hyletic level and precedes consciousness insofar as affectivity is a condition for the possibility of anything coming to appear. Body and psyche are affected before consciousness can turn upon what is given and try to make sense of it. Michel Henry often deploys examples taken from sense experience. Though we may be aware of hearing or seeing something, what we think we hear or see has first been revealed at the level of pre-conscious sensation as an affect.[14] The conscious, objectified, and intentional content of sight and hearing is delayed and comes to appear after consciousness begins to make sense of data given affectively and passively in sensations. Moreover, there are some sensations, for example, pain, that have no object: they are not objectifiable. We simply feel them; we are affected by them. Pain is often described in metaphorical terms: it is sharp, piercing, or dull, but pain itself cannot be objectivated in consciousness as other objects of sensation can be. The experience of pain, of suffering, is isolated by Michel Henry as a unique experience, as it helps us explain how appearing itself occurs: we are beset by an unpleasant and distressing sensation that makes appearing appear without any traditional object other than the awareness or presentation of our own being subjected to suffering (EM 585). In suffering, manifestation or appearing itself can show itself, but concomitant with this very possibility of showing is auto-affection (EM 290–291).

Auto-affection refers to an affective experience in which the self is revealed, not as a conscious ego that wills, decides, reasons, and judges, much like the Cartesian ego; rather, as an experience or sense of ownness or myness that comes to manifest itself through sense-impressions and affects, and is activated by its capacity to undergo affective experiences. Let us turn back to the experience of suffering. In suffering, in what Henry calls pathos, we are beset by and undergo suffering. It is not something we can willingly choose to activate in us, at least at the level of affectivity, Henry claims. I cannot actively will to feel suffering at any point in time, but I can certainly bring about the circumstances that will cause me to suffer; in short, I have to bring about or actively cause the conditions that will make me suffer, but I cannot immediately choose or will the affect of suffering itself. As passion, traditionally, is something that overcomes or besets us—the Latin root of the English word suggests we bear what the passions give—so suffering, too, overwhelms us. What makes appearing possible is our capacity for affectivity, which, when elicited by something, receives or is impressed upon by what is being given. When I am affected by suffering, not only do I become aware of the sensation of suffering, but I am also simultaneously aware that *I am* suffering. An I or a self is awakened by the suffering, an I that is given to itself because it understands the suffering as its own, my own. The experience of ownness that comes to manifest itself in painful suffering makes manifest the possibility of immanence or interiority, which can best be described as the fundamental experience of what it is to be a self (EM 814, 823).

In addition to mineness, the primary experience of affectivity, passively understood, manifests another aspect: what Henry calls life.[15] Life is not simply a series of biological, chemical, and electric processes that allow one to live; rather, he argues that there is a very sensation of living that emerges in affectivity that coincides with the capacity to be affected by sensations and appearing itself. One feels oneself alive and that life courses through one's being. But the feeling of living does not manifest itself as the mineness of selfhood or the affectivity of an embodied sensation; rather, life points to a radical transcendence. Life is not my own; I live it as it is something given to me: I undergo it. Life reveals itself as a more encompassing phenomenon that embraces others, animals, and plants. Life announces that there is something larger of which I am a part that is not reducible to my affectivity, my body, my self, my suffering, all seemingly radical aspects of an immanence. Life points to an other, an outside in which I share, even if it is primarily given in passive affection. It is life that brings things, persons, other living beings into existence; and it is life, argues Henry, that allows one to experience them as distinct from oneself. Life comes to express itself in a collective fashion in art, religion, and politics, all of which are aspects of what Henry generally calls culture.[16]

I would like to claim that in addition to an originary condition of possibility called manifestation, which comes to presence through embodied affectivity, auto-affection, and life, there is also a world. While it is true that in intentional conscious experience, the world comes to be constituted as a series of coherences of sense or a referential totality of meaning, the world is primarily disclosed, I maintain, within Henry's passive view of manifestation, as described above. How so? In the experiences of auto-affection and sensation, a sense of self and being, impressed upon by something trying to manifest itself, shows itself. But both of these primary disclosures also locate us somewhere and in some whole. Stein, Husserl, and the early Heidegger tell us that the world is constituted as some kind of whole of reference. The fundamental experience of a whole can only show itself through various parts that stand in some relation to one another. This is true for sensations and auto-affection. The experience of mineness can only be grasped if it is positioned against something which is not mine. Hegel teaches us this at the beginning of the *Phenomenology of Spirit* in his discussion of the indexical "here" and the "there" that helps consciousness become ever aware of itself. Even in an extreme form of solipsism, various sensations and disclosures of mineness do not simply stand against a background isolated from one another. In fact, we can say that the moment the primary disclosure of auto-affection and sensation occurs, what is given immediately stands in some relation to itself and something that is not itself, immanence and transcendence: the sensations are my sensation, the mineness is my own and not someone else's. These primary aspects configure themselves vis-à-vis one another; relations are formed between self and not self, self and other, immanence and transcendence. It is these fundamental relations that are the building blocks of sense that take on an increased, more intense presence through intentional consciousness and the work of reason and logic, valuing, and judgment.

Let us return to the example of suffering. The pain that one endures makes present the deep layers of the self and sensation that help build up our conscious experience. A spiritual or psychological pain has no real location in the body, yet we see its traces in the body: a sad countenance, for example, or a lack of focus or energy. The pain also manifests that the senses of the self and affection that are passively sedimented in us are not simply isolated aspects: they come to bear on one another as the sensations and the self join to form a world of the I, a surround for the I. The I can only be seen in a horizon, and that horizon is the fundamental locus in which the beginnings of a world take root. In the *Visible and the Invisible*, Maurice Merleau-Ponty remarks, "The thickness of the body, far from rivaling that of the world, is on the contrary the sole means I have to go unto the heart of the things, by making myself a world and by making them flesh."[17] While it is true that Merleau-Ponty is discussing a more conscious form of active constitution, he does announce the possibility of a world that surges with the I. I would like to root the condition of the possibility of the world in a kind of originary positioning, combining, and relationality that is contained within the very structure of manifestation and affectivity itself. One does not simply undergo manifestation and affectivity; rather, manifestation carries with it a mode of its givenness, a quality that comes to expression through the arrangements of the elements of a primary disclosure. The how and where of mineness, affectivity, and perhaps even life are given as standing in relation to one another; they are embedded somewhere—in a horizon, with someone, and somewhere in time—and together they create a relationality and positionality that announce the very condition for the possibility of a world, namely, the fundamental capacity for the interrelationality and intersectionality of affectivity in sensation, auto-affection, and life that allows us, others, and things to be positioned in a whole of sense we call the world. The conscious and intentional mind is not the sole organizer and sense-giver: the layers of sense are already disclosed and made visible through fundamental, transcendental structures that coincide with manifestation itself: affectivity, auto-affection, life, a relational placing and positioning that is the fundamental possibility of a world itself. The philosophical advantage of postulating a passive world and worlding structure that is concomitant with manifestation itself is that we simply do not have a random general giving; rather, we have something given that is positioned from the start, which consciousness can build upon and even change.

Can the fundamental manifestation of the possibility of a world manifest the wholeness of a world? Is a world completely visible? In my view the world can never be disclosed fully, even if worlding itself is a fundamental capacity that manifests itself in and through affectivity. There are two factors that render the world in a partial or limited way, thereby bringing to the fore a certain impossibility. First, following Bergson, the time of creative evolution means that the world and all of reality is in a state of becoming and, therefore, fundamentally incomplete or unfinished. We can experience this sense of becoming within the immediate givens of consciousness. The return to lived-stream of experience has an anticipatory nature to it in that it is always protending, anticipating more content or future meaning. Indeed, this is how the flow of sense is made possible. Furthermore, what is past is no longer. Michel Henry speaks of temporality, especially in its exstases of past, present, and future (EM 448–450), as a fundamental structure that displays the limits of both transcendence and immanence, at least from the standpoint of human consciousness. Because consciousness finds itself temporally conditioned by the work of the past that annihilates that which is present and a future that is constantly anticipating more content of consciousness or experience, what becomes manifest in consciousness and, therefore affectivity, will be limited by the affects of temporality: annihilation and anticipation of something that is not yet. These two effects of time render a full and absolute disclosure of world impossible as the world is being both erased and anticipated in its becoming.

Second, because we are historical beings subjected, in the Foucaultian sense, to the force or power of social and political discourses, both consciously and unconsciously, we have to admit that our sense of the world and our capacity to experience it will be conditioned by these forces and powers. One thinks, for example, of how biopolitics and the governmentality it enforces condition our experience and understanding of what is our own: our bodies, relationality, world, and affectivity. Technology is another example: it conditions our very understanding of ourselves and even our consciousness, which is often described as a computer of sorts. Henry is acutely aware of the forces of economics, history, and technology that shape our capacities to experience ourselves, life, and the world. In fact, in *La barbarie*, he explains how the universities have been completely gutted of any culture-producing possibilities, and taken over by a vision of business, management, and technology that is hostile to human freedom.[18] In the end, a kind of alienation (EM 81–83) settles in that is concomitant with the impossibility of making the world fully present, even though we may desire it or believe consciousness has the capacity to make it so.

For there to be a world means that passive structures that have already made this *world* possible—positioning and relating us to one another, a world that coincides with us and that helps arrange our relations with one another—localize fundamental structures like selfhood, sensibility, and living. A world will live on because it is already being shaped passively and actively by sensations, habits, affects, auto-affection, and life itself, which announces new possibilities, and future becomings. Yet, this world remains unfinished and still to come: its sense and our understanding of it continue to unfold.

Auto-Affection: The Opening onto the Inner Life

The foregoing discussion of *oikeiosis*, auto-affection, and world manifest an important claim: there is a naturally occurring interrelationship between people that is vital for the becoming of the self and finding one's place in the world with others. Political impasse challenges this natural oikeiotic process because it freezes the world and our sense of belonging and being-at-home in the world; a dominant political paradigm takes control of our lives and sense of ourselves, thereby limiting the potential to become. Life and all of its possibilities become precarious, and no natural faith is possible, to borrow a term from the philosopher Thomas Langan.[19] Political impasse affects the sense of who we are, how we stand in relation to others, and the way we experience and create a shared world. I would like to focus more intensely on the affectivity of political impasse and its importance for a greater sense of the self, understood as oikeiotic. I draw upon the work of the French philosopher Michel Henry, to show that the affectivity of political impasse can make manifest the reality of auto-affection, which can bring forth a sense of self that longs to respond to the impasse precisely because the self sees itself as threatened by the situation created by the impasse.

Henry's philosophy of culture has often been employed or cited to further analyze his views on politics, religion, art, education, and ethics.[20] For Henry, culture is the affective "movement of the interior becoming of life"[21] that feels and experiences itself, and which ultimately expands and grows, inspiring and soliciting the desire to respond to that which it lives. These responses, in turn, express or concretize themselves in the ethics, religion, and art of a community. Culture is a movement within the life of subjectivity. The affect moving within us is initially experienced as *pathos,* as something that happens to us—something we bear or suffer.

Here, we discover that there is more to us than we know: there is Life. Life is not reducible to our consciousness of it, but it is the very condition for the possibility of all being, including what is most precious to traditional phenomenology—intentionality, manifestation, and sense. Life structures us such that we begin to feel, to experience ourselves and our own lives, in initial bodily impressions given to us through the senses: what Husserl calls *Empfindungen*. That we experience sensations is given, but we do so primarily in a passive mode, as *pathos*. We also experience sensations that originate within ourselves. Sensations affect us and the affects to which sensations give rise produce a reflexive consciousness about the sensations themselves and about our own subjectivity and life. It is this initial and primary move that opens the larger structure of our lives and Life in general, which primarily manifests itself within our interiorities. An interior life is revealed, a life that becomes thicker with meaning and lived experience, a life that enables us to build worlds and to constitute a sense of ourselves and of things in the world. But, for Henry, not only do we give sense to worlds and objects that lie outside ourselves, we also shape and form an interior world or life, unique to the individual, which is also shared as communal insofar as human beings can express their interior life through language, art, religion, and ethics.[22]

We begin to feel, to live ourselves, in our immanence or immanent being. Culture, for Henry, begins in a profound passivity that receives and bears the effects of one's life and the living-through of oneself—what Henry calls auto-affection. In short, this auto-affection generates the profound realization that we are living, but that we also live within ourselves. The more that is given to us in our material bodies through sensations or sense-impressions, the more we have to reflect upon and the more we begin to expand our interior lives; this is part of what Henry calls auto-donation.[23] As layers of meaning or sense are added to this affective level, a desire for the interior life to transform itself and grow develops. It enacts this growth or enhancement, this becoming, through the Husserlian *Ich kann* or "I can." Henry claims we can see the expression of this free play of desire in ethics, religion, and art. Again, the primary affect of life living itself in us and through us is blocked in and by a state of impasse. The impasse dominates our lives and interiority.

Traditionally, we understand culture as the objects of art, religion, and ethics, but, for Henry, this objective, phenomenological description is woefully inadequate as these objects, when viewed merely as products, occlude the very source of culture from manifesting itself—Life, especially the becoming of the interior life.[24] Moreover, if we examine the more traditional, subjective accounts of culture provided, for example, by Hegel—one of Henry's main interlocutors—culture emerges at a given historical moment in human consciousness; it marks a specific moment in the life of spirit as it becomes fully aware of itself and moves dialectically toward objective spirit.

In the *Phenomenology of Spirit*, Hegel places culture between ethics and morality. The former deals with a way of being (*ethos*) or the character of an individual or individuals, whereas the latter deals with duty *vis-à-vis* what is understood to be good or bad. In paragraph 489 of the *Phenomenology*, Hegel remarks:

> It is therefore through culture that the individual acquires standing and actuality. His true original nature and substance is the alienation of himself as Spirit from his natural being. This externalization is, therefore, both the purpose and the existence of the individual; it is at once the means, or the transition, both of the [mere] thought-form of substance into actuality, and conversely, of the specific

individuality into essentiality. This individuality moulds itself by culture into what it intrinsically is, and only by doing so is it an intrinsic being that has an actual existence; the measure of its culture is the measure of its actuality and power. Although here the self knows itself as this self, yet its actuality consists solely in the setting-aside of its natural self.[25]

First, Hegel sees culture as a process of self-consciousness or self-actualization. Culture is a stage of knowing *en route* to an *absolutes Wissen* or "absolute knowing." For Henry, Life is prior to and more conditioning than consciousness itself; Life is truly transcendent, whereas consciousness cannot account for, at least in strict phenomenological terms, the very possibility of and condition for its manifestation in consciousness.

Second, culture is generally understood as the moment in which an individual grasps herself as an individual and comprehends how she can shape herself in and through this culture. The individual is determined not merely as she is according to ethics, as a character possessing certain definable qualities that, to borrow Hegel's language, stem from external sources, including "natural" determinations of character, custom, and legal right. It is in culture that the individual, argues Hegel, becomes aware of how she can shape herself in and through her own self-activation in the world. Culture, then, becomes a self-shaping through one's conscious awareness of oneself as no longer determined merely by outside natural forces, such as law and the character or *ethos* of a particular set of individuals. In concrete terms, one moves from the histories of Thucydides and Herodotus, in which an individual is shaped by the customs and habits of the Greek world, to Socrates, a Greek Athenian who is also aware of how he can be uniquely Socrates—the lover of wisdom, the philosopher, the wisest of men, who knows that he does not know. Greek philosophy is itself an example of culture—a culture that informed Athenian life and shaped the self-understanding of the individual at a certain moment in history.

For Henry, this account, which progresses in stages of self-awareness that become increasingly intense and, therefore, increasingly self-shaping and determining, is too teleological. Henry is also troubled by the primacy of consciousness for it assumes an absolute identity, progressive as it is, between the knower and the object known or, to employ Husserlian language, the *noesis* and the *noema*. This identity is not grounded in itself for Henry; rather, it is made possible through intentionality. At a deeper level, it is also made manifest from a nonintentional source. Culture can arise only when a more original force—what Henry calls Life—impresses itself upon an individual life that chooses to respond to this impression, this profound pathos. This response to Life's pathos is the source of culture that makes us aware of ourselves. Culture is not an idiopsychic or auto-referential process. For Henry, culture cannot be idiotic; if it becomes so, by ignoring Life and the impressions it yields upon the individual life, it begins to die. Unlike Hegel, who views culture very much within identitarian terms (i.e., the "essential" self-identification of the subject as subject and source of culture), Henry wishes to preserve the transcendent source of culture which is Life.

An explanation of the background and analysis of Henry's position would entail the exposition of his phenomenology; space does not permit such an endeavor here. Rather, I would like to focus on his views of culture, as well as his critique of scientific or Galilean culture before returning to my primary argument concerning impasse. There are three key, constitutive moments in Henry's account of culture: auto-revelation, auto-affection, and auto-enhancement (*auto-accroissement*). Throughout his *œuvre*, Henry consistently argues that if we study the nature of consciousness closely, our conscious awareness manifests the plain fact that it is not self-contained or self-positing, understood in the Fichtean sense. Dan Zahavi notes,

> According to Henry, one of the characteristic features of Husserl's and Heidegger's classical investigations has been their emphasis on the self-transcending nature of appearance; no appearance is independent and self-reliant. It always refers to something different from itself. On the one hand, every appearance is characterized by a dyadic structure; it is an appearance of something for someone. Every appearance has its genitive and its dative. On the other hand, every appearance is characterized by its horizontality, that is, by its reference to a plurality of other appearances.[26]

The very possibility of consciousness, then, has its roots in a deeper reality, namely, Life. Henry always distinguishes lives and how we each live our lives phenomenologically from Life or *Vie* in general, which is Henry's name for the whole or totality in which we dwell.

Henry employs the prefix "auto" to define a self-reflexive movement. When he claims that Life is prior to consciousness, especially as this is revealed in his analyses of passivity and *Empfindungen*, which together he calls *pathos*,[27] he insists that Life manifests itself to itself. Life is not deduced or confirmed by empirical experiments; it transcends our very attempts to determine and verify it, albeit this does not mean we cannot know anything about it. Life manifests itself as primordially given, and it is in this sense that we are to understand it as self-revealing: it gives itself to consciousness, both as subjectively embodied and as a larger totality. But life is not a simple monad, that is, it is not to be understood as a substance; rather, it is differentiated and reveals itself in a plurality of particular forms. In fact, one never sees Life itself, but only its particular manifestations, including subjectivity, animal life, physical objects, and phenomena. Zahavi remarks:

> To claim that self-manifestation involves division, separation, and opposition is according to Henry to fall victim to one basic misunderstanding. A misunderstanding that has dominated most of Western thought, and which Henry has dubbed the ontological monism. This is Henry's term for the assumption that there is only one type of manifestation, only one type of phenomenality. Thus it has been taken for granted, that to be given, to appear, was always to be given as an object. Needless to say, it is exactly this principle of ontological monism which has been behind the persisting attempts to interpret self-awareness in terms of reflection or introspection. The model of intentionality has been the paradigm; self-awareness has been understood as the result of an objectifying, intentional activity, and self-manifestation therefore as a special form of inner object-manifestation, characterized by horizontality, duality and transcendence.[28]

Life is given in such a way that it simultaneously constitutes the ground or condition for the possibility of all that is, but it also manifests itself in a variety of forms, from the rock to the human being. One is reminded here of the opening sections of Husserl's *Ideas II*, in which the description of various forms of *zoa* or biological life are given sense. One particular aspect of the essence of life is its capacity to be aware of itself, especially at the primary level of affectivity. Life, claims Henry, is auto-affective or self-feeling and, in this sense, it is pathetic or capable of receiving impressions. Henry's discussion of human affectivity as experienced through sense-impressions shows this process. Human beings, even before they are aware of higher subjectivities and objectivities, especially social ones, are aware of having sense-impressions. These impressions do not bespeak an I or a lived experience of a body; rather, they signify sensation and the condition of being affected, a primordial passivity. Our conscious experience and our capacity to make sense of our experience are conditioned by our basic capacity to be affected. Life affects itself, and the more it continues to do so at various points and levels of interaction, the more it becomes. There are layers of complexity, from the lowest awareness—the capacity to be affected by sense-impressions—to higher, complex structures, such as acts of will and culture. For Henry, the auto-affection of life both subjectivates and objectivates; that is, it can produce deeper and richer notions of subjectivity as well as objectivity.[29] Phenomenology studies the various processes and constitutive senses of life as life affects itself in its various forms, including the specifically human form of the person, individually and communally, which comprises art, culture, and politics. More precisely, various forms of cultural expression not only embody the spirit of a people, but also the expression of Life in general. The very incarnation of a culture in a people and the way in which they live out this culture is the expression of Life and its auto-affection. Such is the nature of Life.

As Life lives itself in its plurality of forms, senses, and expressions, it is given the possibility of enhancing itself and, I should also say, of destroying itself. When we choose to stop the process of Life's self-development or self-enhancement, we have what Henry calls barbarism.[30] Let me better situate our discussion of Life by framing it within Henry's discussion of culture. As previously mentioned, culture is Henry's term for a specific incarnation of life, namely, its capacity to affect itself and thereby produce an inner life or interiority. This interiority has a shape and is seen as the place where, through our freedom (*Ich kann*) and desire, we can give form and sense to the deepest structures of being, including our being and our humanity. This auto-affection of a life that is given feels itself and creates itself into a particular "thing," such as a human person or a subject.[31] Indeed, the becoming of our interior world allows us to shape our outer world, and to give it sense.[32] In creating such forms, in the very becoming of interiority (i.e., culture), Life experiences or lives itself in particular forms. Henry claims that the essence of Life is to continue to grow and become more complex, as well as to diversify. The various expressions of our rich human interiorities are affirmed by the numerous and rich cultures that currently exist and that have existed throughout the world's history. These cultures contain language, myth, poetry, science, politics, and art which are all part of the inner life of a group of people, all part of Life coming to express and feel itself. Henry describes art as the sustained work of affect: in her own life, the artist bears the impressions not only of herself but also of Life, and she responds deeply to both through the work she produces. This work is the concretization or manifestation of an aspect of both her own life and of Life in the more encompassing, holistic sense. What the artist lives, according to Henry, is the deep impression of her own auto-affection as well as her being affected by Life. Art is not merely a product of this affect, but it is also an extension or manifestation of life-/Life-lived, as well as of the Living that makes possible our own specific life. Henry takes up this argument in his work on Kandinsky, in which he argues that line and color can allow us to move away from visible form to see the work of the invisible essence of Life.[33]

Today, Henry claims, the very possibility of the becoming of the interior world, which is culture, is under threat; we are in an impasse as life itself has been colonized by the powers of technology and business. Drawing on Husserl and his critique of science, especially as developed in his *Crisis,* Henry argues that our present-day world has been shaped by an emphasis on external, objective, and empirical verification. He traces this orientation to early modern thinking, especially that of Galileo, in which reality is understood in two fundamental ways.[34] First, there is what Galileo calls matter—physical reality. But this view of unified matter is something of which we are a part and is not specific to human beings. In many ways, the Galilean view of matter exceeds human subjectivity. Our subjectivity is formed and conditioned by this more foundational and encompassing sense of matter. We are subject to matter that exists outside our own interiority; indeed, our interiority may be part of this larger sense of matter.

Second, and more importantly, Henry claims that Galileo mathematizes reality. With the introduction of Galilean physics, reality becomes understood and measurable through mathematical relations. An abstraction occurs insofar as we use the ideal language of mathematics to express what actually is and what lies outside language itself. This new scientific attitude, according to Henry, bespeaks a contradiction[35] because, on the one hand, science uses certain language, ideas, and formulae to measure and describe reality but, on the other hand, it can give no account of its own language or, especially, of its origins. Moreover, claims Henry, the Galilean or scientific description of reality is identified with reality itself: reality is reduced to what science can measure, verify, and report. The scientist observes, measures, and discovers what is from a purely objective or external position. And though science can certainly describe what it seeks as externally present—that is, free from subjective relativity, prejudice, and error—it is a mistake to claim this is reality. The scientific attitude reduces reality to the external.

What is forgotten, and what takes precedence for Henry, is the very living-through, within the intimacy and life of the individual subject or communities of subjects, of what science discovers and knows. The Galilean scientific attitude forgets that which conditions and is prior to its own analyses and study of objective phenomena, namely, Life. Let us pause for a brief moment to unpack these claims. The reality that science claims to uncover, measure, understand, and use technologically is presented as some object that lies over and against us; we observe it and study it as an object that is not us.[36] Henry claims, however, that subjectivity is most intimately constituted and first lived within our own interiority. Reality is given to us in our own inner lives, and it first appears as that auto-affection discussed earlier. Reality is thus first lived passively, and as we begin to reflect upon and experience it intensely—live it—within our own inner lives, we give sense to it. "Culture is the collection of undertakings and practices in which the superabundance of life expresses itself; all of these have as their motivation the 'charge,' the 'excess' that interiorly disposes living subjectivity as a force ready to be prodigious."[37] What the scientific attitude denies, negates, or abstracts from is the primacy of the lived experience of reality and the world that is contained, expressed, and developed by the interior life, focusing instead on the object of scientific investigation, reducing our lives and Life to our own concepts and created externalized objects. Through the auto-affection that makes one conscious of life and of one's body and all that it feels, Henry claims one also discovers that, prior to consciousness and prior to science, it is Life that enables and conditions both the living of our reflexive interior lives and science.[38] Life is the transcendental condition for the possibility of culture, which is nothing other than the singular and collective expression of our interior lives in art, religion, and ethics, which are distinct and separate from science.[39]

Henry claims that, concomitant with the scientific attitude, our overemphasis on the primacy of the external as charting and mapping the interior life is strengthened and reinforced by diverse forms of media, bad Freudianism, and the failure of the university system to cultivate a rich inner life that would permit subjectivity and culture to thrive. The barbarism that Henry refers to entails the fact that there has been a concerted effort to negate and deny the being and development of an inner life distinct from the scientific life of objectivity, especially in the administrative and quantifying cultures that dominate universities as well as in the representational life of the media, and the unconscious, subjectless life of bad Freudianism, which results in an uprooted, unconscious life that has no connection to a conscious inner life.[40] The result is an auto-negation or auto-destruction of life itself, of the thing that, according to Henry, must be understood as the very condition for the possibility of science and culture.

Henry aptly captures an aspect of our experience of a stream of Western culture which colonizes and dominates through a strong belief in technology, efficiency, and capitalism, and ultimately leads to the stymying, the killing of life, thereby contributing to the sense of political impasse that many feel today. Political life, especially as it is internally felt and lived, cannot come forward. Can we uncover the primary and sustaining feeling of life that allows us to individuate ourselves and our interiority, building a culture and world, such that we can recover a means to respond to the impasse from within? I believe we can.

Self-Becoming: To Feel and Live Oneself Anew?

The first step to dealing with political impasse is to recognize and admit that we have reached a blocked state of being in which self and shared world are severely compromised; the pressure this blockage exerts on us makes us feel the presence of the impasse, but as Henry shows us we also feel the presence of a living self that experiences itself as coming to be in and through reflexive experience while enduring this impasse. The second step involves a willful decision to struggle with oneself, to labor with and against oneself. One must enact a caesura with the self that is generated and structured by the matrix of financial capital, technology, and oligarchy. This is very difficult to do because, once one does or even ponders doing so, one finds that the self that is supposed to be there—the self that one wants to be present—is not: it has been so thoroughly overdetermined from the outside that the process of *oikeiosis* has been absorbed by this matrix. If we turn inward to try and see the self, the self of liberal politics, for example, most of us have to admit that such a self is not evident or apparent. Our task is to make it appear, so that we can think new ideas and see new visions of ourselves that, in turn, extend outward to reform that which is causing the blockage of our own political wills. Arendt invites us inward when, following Augustine, she remarks, "Whoever wishes to say 'I am,' and to summon up his own unity and identity and put it against the variety and multiplicity of the world, must withdraw himself into some inner region, turning his back on whatever the 'outside' can offer."[41]

But to turn away completely from the outside is impossible, for we find ourselves between an inner and outer world. The world continues to impact and shape us. It would seem that what we need to do is restore the relationship between the inner world of self-becoming and the outside world, a world that includes human creation and is marked by our spontaneity, imagination, and desire. Today's world of political impasse is the extension of the self-interest of a few powerful people. The political world in which we dwell is designed by others that have subjugated us and domesticated our own self-becoming: we are like trained animals in the circus. We respond only to the empty promises and material goods delivered by the few in charge, partly, perhaps, because we have nothing of an inner life to oppose the subjugation: our oikeiotic interiors remain blocked and colonized. Undoubtedly, and this is important, the oikeiotic response I discuss here is one of many possible responses to impasse. It would be naïve and plain wrong to argue that what is being proposed here is the only solution or appropriate countermove to impasse; rather, it is one possibility among many. For example, Iris Marion Young reminds us that in a deep sense we are all responsible for the global injustice that plagues us, that is, we bear the collective burden of responsibility of trying to stop them, while seeking to make a better, more just world. Moving away from a direct liability model of injustice, Young views the social connection model as a way to move forward, to move beyond impasse, if you will.[42] Likewise, Arendt reminds us that in many ways we are responsible for the regimes that we have in place. Regimes stay in place because of the support they receive from the populace. Undoing our complicity, standing against it and breaking it, certainly is a way to respond to a crisis of political impasse. Again, like Foucault, Deleuze, and Esposito, discussed above, the move to deal with the impasse certainly does include a move to self-recognition, but once this moment of consciousness is grasped, we turn to the outside external circumstances that need to be changed. What I am arguing for here, in a moment when a turn to the outside is not possible, is a reconfiguration of the self, from within—a shifting and reconfiguration of the self that can think or imagine oneself, the world, and others in a different way. It is not only the outer structures of social and political life that need to be shifted but also the internal, subjective ones.

The call inward is not a retreat or withdrawal, but a temporary move to become aware of the reins that control us. But we must not remain only in our interiority for the self requires intimate contact with the world and others to thrive. This is the foundation of politics. The intimacy must be restored and reconceived, not as an indifferent privacy, but as a genuine human exchange aimed at our own flourishing—our collective flourishing that is not simply reduced to bare subsistence. The French sociologist and philosopher, Jacques Ellul, prophetically noted in his 1977 *The Technological Society* that what is dangerous and deadly about post–Second World War capitalism was the changing notion of necessity: today, what we conceive of as necessary for good life in common is largely exaggerated and colored with extravagant desires for entertainment and real estate. Aristotle's "goods of the soul" have no place in our contemporary model of business politics. Necessity has become the stuff of human capitalist desires. If we turn inward, at least for a while, we must also be aware that we will need to exit this inner world to transform the outer world of politics. Augustine was right to claim that we must return to ourselves, *in te redi*, but he also urges us to restore the world, especially the human city in which we live together communally and politically.

One of the important words used in Greek philosophy to express the "constitution" or state of being of a city-state is *politeia*. Aristotle's *Politics* chronicles the various *politeia* of city-states, and compares them to figure out which would achieve the best kind of collective human flourishing. Plato employs the term to signify a way of being in the city-state. In the *Republic*, we see his full-scale contempt for the rule of the Thirty Tyrants, as well as his contempt for democracy. In his ideal state, our common well-being is thought through in a hierarchical fashion; he divides society into three classes: workers and craftsmen, guardians, and the philosopher-king. To live well together, according to Plato, is to have a *politeia* that follows his prescriptions for political order and ultimately produces a deep sense of justice that permeates all of society. Recall that justice, for Plato, is rooted in everyone and everything in the cosmos doing what it is supposed to do. In short, our way of being together must be just if we are to progress as a city-state. The way of being for a political regime today does have a profound effect on us. My claim that it can produce a sense of fatalism stemming from a deep experience of political impasse means no real *politeia* exists; we have only *apoliteia*.

What is fascinating about *apoliteia* is that it is essentially a passive structure: it overcomes us and we have no control over it. In many ways, it mimics an uncontrollable passion to which we succumb. Our interiority, the place where we begin to think through the state of political impasse, has a deep, passive structure. It bears the impressions of the world and other human beings, as well as that of the self, including the effects of emotion, thought, deeds, the unconscious, will, and varying kinds of decisions. As *apoliteia* overcomes us, entrenching itself in our person, it causes these affects. Stoic and neo-Stoic philosophers recognized that humans have very little control over the impressions we receive or that inflict themselves on us, but we do have some control over how we deal with their effects. We must come to know, through discipline and exercise, these effects, and we must learn how to either enjoy, prevent, or simply bear them. Good reasoning and judgment can assist us in making such distinctions.

It is important to state here that moments of political impasse have a deep passive form, but they are momentary, that is, they occur in time and for a certain moment of time. History has shown us this. We cannot treat political impasse as concomitant with a trenchant notion of unyielding fate. This being said, we do experience momentary periods of fate: we are doomed in this time to remain mired in impasse.

To simply say that the future will bring us better things is to bank on future possibilities, which inevitably runs the risk of reinforcing the burden of the fatalism that accompanies political impasse. We must seize the wisdom of the Stoics and recognize that we do indeed have some freedom, despite the overwhelming feeling of being subjected to a state of affairs that we cannot control. We do still have some freedom to begin to think our predicament anew. We must do so by reclaiming the active freedom we have in thinking through affects of *apoliteia*.

Undoubtedly, the heaviest burden of *apoliteia* is its affective dimension, namely the feeling of impotence to change things, lethargy, futility, despair, and abandon. These feelings are precisely that—feelings. Our interior lives are larger than our affective capacities. We are also imagining, thinking, and judging beings, and these distinct capacities can and do work independently from our emotive capacities. In recognizing this larger interior framework, we also realize that we do have freedom, a freedom to invoke what Nietzsche called *Trotzmacht*, the "power to act despite." In this case, we choose to explore other facets of our interior lives, despite the overwhelming sensations of futility.

In times of political impasse, the material and political circumstances either create situations of profound cyclicality or repetition, much like the scenes of violence and vengeance described by the Greek tragedians, or a blockage in which nothing moves. What other facets of our interior lives offer genuine possibilities that can help us bear the impasse in which we find ourselves while creating new possibilities for a genuine politics—a veritable *politeia*? I venture the following interior capacities: thinking, imagining, judging, and willing, each of which has the potential to move, even when the material and situational experiences of political life make physical change seemingly impossible. Thinking otherwise may be an almost nothing (a *presque rien*) that is virtually *en route* to something else, to borrow an insight from Vladimir Jankélévitch: the beginning of a possibility to be otherwise, politically and materially. An insight may shine forth that may affect our psychic and mental circumstances.

Thinking

In the living or being at-home of *oikeiosis*, one finds the freedom to think. Arendt conceived of thinking as an appearing or making manifest something new: thought makes things appear to the mind. Traditionally, thinking has been understood as calculative or rational; it computes, organizes, and even reasons about the objects it holds before it. Deduction and inference can be made in thinking, all bespeaking a logical capacity of the mind. And while it is true that thinking indeed performs these functions, it also contemplates. The root sense of the word "conversation" is to turn things around and around: thinking is a conversation one has with oneself. But even this definition falls short: thinking gives precedence to the object or the content of the mind. The French philosopher Pierre Hadot conceives of the conversation with oneself in much broader terms. Reading the work of Marcus Aurelius,[43] Hadot observes that thinking also produces an effect on the self. We are affected by our thoughts of and in the impasse, and it is the effect of thought on ourselves that we tend to neglect. He argues that Marcus Aurelius understood this deep, affective structure in a unique way, and his specific contribution to philosophy was the argument that we need exercises and disciplines to limit the sometimes-noxious affects of thought itself.

What gives thought its force, to borrow an expression from both Kant and Nietzsche, is the effect produced when one knows that something is true or right. It is not the seized object of thought itself that moves us, but the effect it has on us. The conversation with oneself engenders an effect on the self that underlies the conversation. There are then two selves, a classic position in the understanding of thought as a conversation taken up by ancient authors like Augustine. The idea of the self as an identity of certainty comes much later with the advent of modern philosophy. The Ancients were very much at home with this bifurcated self that is not wholly defined by a unity cast into a modern framework of autonomy or self-activation (*Selbsttätigkeit*). The effect that the conversation of thought produces in us is revelatory and this is where the power of thinking begins. The revelation, of course, can happen only when one disciplines the mind to be attentive to what one undergoes in both the conversation and the effects of the conversation. It is largely true that, in the West, philosophers have taught us to ignore or dismiss the effects of this conversation. More recent studies in analytic philosophy, thankfully, have shown that there is a rationality to the emotions—they are not simply passions. But even this account privileges a certain kind of thinking that is drenched with calculative utility.

What is revealed in the affect of thinking? If one resists the temptation to dismiss the affective structure of the conversation of thought, one becomes aware of a whole passive repository of life (what Augustine understood as memory) that grounds the life of the self. Edith Stein sees this background as a self of collected reflections, a *positum*, a place where actions, ideas, experiences, and traumas are stored and sedimented. For Stein, the self is built from this passive *positum*, whereas the I is the waking or I of consciousness; the I is both the zero point of orientation of consciousness and the agent that focuses consciousness. The conversation of thought draws upon that which is collected in ourselves—all that has gone into or remains in the very making of selves as humans in time. This is the more substantial side of the self as it perdures somewhat in time. The actual conversation is a short duration, but it requires the more durational notion of the self that is stored and comes to the fore through the selections of memory.

The substantial self of memory is that which constantly accumulates and forgets experiences and understandings of ourselves: the self holds these memories and experiences in place to help shape what we understand by identity, selfhood, or the response to the question of Who am I? The activity of the conversation mobilizes parts of the substantial self to either affirm what it already understands the self to be, undo what the self is, or simply continue to add layers that perhaps will never be accessed: an unfinished self or a self that is in progress, and which may never come to be. The conversation can help reveal the ground that accumulates and acts as the resting spot of experience that gives sense to the self. Let us consider an example: I may find myself facing a certain ethical dilemma. The conversation of the self certainly has the dilemma as its subject, but as I begin to toss the object of thought around in my mind, trying to understand it and figure out its implications, looking for a solution to the predicament, each singular thought I have about the dilemma impresses itself against the background of consciousness, my past experiences, and beliefs, and if

I am attentive, a certain affect is produced. The affect indicates that, at a deep, even preconscious level, some kind of decision or insight has already happened.

Not only do we need to question the object of our conversation then, but also why the conversation affects us in the way it does. What is in our background that allows us to have the reactions we do? Could it be that something is also revealed through the affect of the conversation about our backgrounds? I venture that, yes, something is happening and something is being revealed about ourselves. Our task is now to bring it forward through the power of imagination and to work with judgment to see whether it can assist us in thinking through the dilemma. We will further discuss imagination and judgment later. In short, the affect reveals something about ourselves and who we are, especially when confronted by the dilemma we find ourselves in. Deeper self-understanding requires that we mine this affective structure of thought that is revealed in the conversation we have with ourselves and the objects that impress themselves on us in our dwelling in the world and with others. The affects of thought bounce up against an inner world, a repository of experiences, much of which have been synthesized and organized to give sense to ourselves. Our identity resides or is conserved in this *positum* of life and our experiences. Active impressions created by thought and our interaction with the world and others are absorbed by this repository and we try to make sense of them. This being said, it would be dishonest not to point out that, in addition to memories and senses that surge forward, there are also vast swaths of the unconscious that recede and will perhaps never come to the fore.

How Does Thinking Affect Political Impasse?

I believe we can all agree there are conversations something like the one I have described, but we need to concentrate on the passive repository, for it is here that we find something like self or personal identity. By focusing on this aspect of our being, we also uncover a world or a sense of the world in which we dwell. The heavy emphasis on thought as action or activity gives it a temporal duration that is caught up in instantaneity. We think now and our thinking is always forward looking, if we continue to see it in very active, calculative terms. If we unpack thought's affective, passive structures, we find sense and sedimentation of the self and our reception of the world. This is not to say that the deposited self is fixed or unchanging; rather, it simply has greater duration, albeit temporal and finite. It somehow persists longer than the very present activity of thinking in a series of now moments.

So, how do this inner sedimented world and sense of the self relate to political impasse? The *apoliteia* of political impasse strikes and impresses itself upon us, and we begin to think actively about it and how it unfolds. Our awareness and thought of political impasse also has an affect on us, which makes accessible the repository against which the affect of thought strikes and emerges. Thinking is absorbed into the repository of the self and new senses are given in response to the impasse. We see that political impasse has been with us for a while and that resistance is futile, at least at this moment. But what is most important about the combination of active thinking on the impasse and the repository of the self is the advent of new possibilities: we can think otherwise. Impasse, we realize, is only a given political moment. We can think of times when there was nothing like impasse, but still a genuine politics. We can begin to reflect on what made those periods of politics so successful in the sense that human beings advanced, and they valued human flourishing over self-interest and greed. To think otherwise is the purpose of the conversation between the active and passive aspects of thought. We cannot easily replicate the conditions that cause flourishing—an age is more than the sum of its parts—but past strategies might be recovered that, when they are reworked and revitalized, fit the contemporary situation of impasse.

To think otherwise is a sign of human freedom insofar as we become aware that the necessity of a given moment of impasse need be neither eternal nor absolute. Moreover, thinking also restores some form of agency; the possibilities are given to us in thought. We need to give to them a more active voice—turn them around and around in thoughtful conversation. To think otherwise is one of the crucial powers of thinking, but it does not necessarily arise spontaneously; it is cultivated through a sustained examination of the encounter between active thought and its more enduring repository in the inner self. But thought alone is not enough to bring about some concrete and imaginative response to political impasse. We require the imagination to extend possibilities that arise in thinking otherwise. The imagination allows us to see newness that stems from realizing we can think otherwise. Imagination allows these new possibilities to take on a new shape, a reworked shape, or even a slight modified form of something that already exists. The greater the exposure to ideas and experiences, the greater the repertoire from which the imagination can draw. And once we have grasped what the imagination brings forward, it urges us to enact it or, at least, contemplate its possible concretion or actualization or even its dismissal as a possibility. The imagination is active—it helps bring forward images and fantasies of new possibilities—but it also has a passive aspect: it affects us, indicating which possibilities are more interesting for us and which we care more about. In many ways, the affect of the imagination incites desires for new possibilities and these possibilities come with differing intensities. We must use judgment to distinguish between the possibilities that present themselves; we must judge which to follow and which to abandon. The will then chooses between the differing intensities, pushes them to completion, and translates them to action.

Imagination

Let us turn to a closer examination of the imagination and its possibilities during impasse. Historically, philosophers conceived of the imagination in three constructive ways. First, it was understood as a kind of mediating force, bringing together sense-impressions and the reactions and work of the psyche to and on those impressions. The Ancients called the products of this interaction or mediation *phantasmata*. These *phantasmata* were literally images of a particular synthesis of what was given by the outside through sense-impressions and the work of the soul which would make visible what those sense-impressions communicated about the world. *Phantasmata* were imaginary objects or representations of what was outside, but some argued they were exact copies or simply appearances. We can understand imagination, in this sense, as synthetically representational. Second, the imagination was considered a power of faculty in its own right. It not only produced images, as in the first sense, but also created new objects which were, in part, drawn from the syntheses. It is this kind of imagination that helped bring forward new works of art, music, philosophy, and science. And, finally, there is the more contemporary sense of the imagination, deeply informed by Romantic as well as twentieth-century psychology, as the locus of pure spontaneity, genuine innovation, and playful creation. This realm of imagination produces fantasy—a domain that intimately influences and structures our lives, from rich social and political imaginaries to pleasant and sometimes painful escapes or flights of fancy.

I do not wish to deny these accounts of imagination as I think they are true. But thinking, understood as a capacity to think otherwise, must be distinguished from imagination which also has an affective structure, and it is this that I believe is crucial for understanding its force. Traditional accounts of the imagination in philosophy privilege presencing: the imagination makes appear, and either a representational synthesis or something new is made visible. Thinking, I believe, can do this too, but the affective power of imagination, which feeds our thinking otherwise, gives it the vital strength to continue by allowing us to see the consequences of our thinking otherwise. But what does this mean?

As we find ourselves existing in political impasse, we feel pressure to retreat inward as external circumstances seem stagnant and unable to nourish any kind of meaningful life. We are stuck. Thinking about possible alternatives to the impasse is a particular labor of our interiority. It helps us articulate alternative possibilities and yields potential self-understanding. The imagination takes what appears and gives it force, moving us from the work of possibility to a feeling of reality. We feel as if what is before us is real and living: it makes things alive before our eyes. The imagination is that which vivifies that which thinking makes apparent, and as it vivifies "as real" what lies before us, thought begins to unfold its deeper resources. Imagination gives to the interiority a palpable reality, even for an instant, that we feel as real; we are affected by the life that imagination imbues into our thought-things. The affect of experiencing our interior possibilities as now, as real, as before us, as living, entices us to want to externalize and share what we have experienced as living. This is the profound affect of the imagination on thought. Without this, our thoughts simply remain objects, things that lie before us. Furthermore, while it is true that both thinking and imagination can help us see the consequences and subsequent possibilities that appear as these two human capacities unfold, there is a fundamental difference in the way they accomplish this. Thinking allows us to see future possibilities and consequences in calculative, strategic ways; Thucydides and Greek physicians used to call this kind of thinking or seeing kairotic. The imagination, however, brings to light new, what seem to be spontaneously generated, options and consequences. It allows us to experience as real never-before-experienced possibilities, usually followed by a deep sense of joy and rapture, what we could call the feeling of genuine inspiration.

We can understand both thinking and imagination as anticipatory, forward-looking structures that open up future possibilities. Thinking brings these new possibilities forward and imagination imbues them with a sense of life, freshness, and tangible graspability. It also causes us to feel the urgency of externalizing what is before us. Thinking, however, rests within the realm of the ego, the *solus ipse* of the conversation that is thought.

We desire to share what imagination makes us feel as real. Externalization not only gives interiority a certain look, what the Greeks called an *eidos* and what we understand as an idea, but it automatically communicates it to the outside world. Our bodies are transformed by the affects of the imagination and thinking otherwise, but we also create and communicate things. We concretize that which we have seen in our interiority either by producing objects, describing them to others, or simply enjoying the affect of what we have experienced. The genuine experience of thinking and imagination is ecstatic—we are removed from our habitual way of being and taken to a world that can be, which we have tasted, but is not fully realized. It has only begun to be. The externalization gives it another look, another form or aspect that is now communicable. Others can now share in what we have experienced. Others can also now contribute to building (or sometimes, sadly, destroying) what we have given birth to in our interiorities.

This is how political visions become realized; they are not merely responses to given situations. Even the most diehard pragmatist must think and imagine. This is where it begins. One of the most dangerous aspects of the combination of technology and financial capital with pragmatic-utilitarian thinking is that it seeks to systematically destroy the potential of thinking and imagination to bring forward alternative possibilities. Our current impasse is experienced as a blockage for those subject to a certain kind of political rule. But the institutions or players that control large capital and resources, the new bourgeoisie, have a vested interest in making sure that thinking and imagination are severely delimited and controlled. They wish to preserve and expand the status quo, both ideological and material, that they have created. Their strategy is not one of targeted control of media and educational systems; rather, it consists of simply generating more goods and services, so much so that, overwhelmed with choices, the population becomes distracted. All is truly entertainment, understood in the sense of *divertissement*, a diversion from serious thinking and imagination. We see this turn gaining momentum in the university and we have to ask ourselves: Why has more university education for more people produced a supposedly educated population that generally reads at a lower level than it did some fifty years ago? Those that complete a university education today have not read as extensively or at the same level as previous generations. One can see this decline in the humanities in which course reading lists feature short excerpts from a variety of texts rather than whole books. Expectations are much lower, thereby producing a less-literate population that, nonetheless, claims to be more highly educated.

The global financial capitalists have done their calculus well: give the population more kinds of bread and a plethora of circus entertainments for these will keep it stupefied and tired. It will be unable to resist the ideological and material takeover of a new political order, in which the people no longer control the politics and economics of their own nations. When Antoine Roquentin complains in Sartre's *Nausea* that he is besieged by too much stuff, what we can understand as the stuff of existence, he at least feels depressed, miserable, and anxious, whereas our contemporary reaction to too much stuff is one of boredom and a desire for more distraction. But the distraction takes us away from our own interiorities; it alienates us and enforces alienating us and enforcing the impasse of too much stuff that we can no longer control and which leads to the death of a genuine political alternative.

Judgment

We now move on to judgment and its relationship to our inward turn. Traditionally, judgment is seen in two fundamental ways. The Ancient Greeks, especially the Stoics, thought of judgment as a process of sorting and selecting they called, along with Aristotle, *prohairesis*: when thinking about a solution for a specific problem, the mind presents various options and, in conjunction with reason, sifts through the possibilities to choose the best one. Judgment, with the aid of reason, guides action; it is not simply a rational deduction or inference—it is intimately linked with doing. The second, no less popular view of judgment is offered by Immanuel Kant. Here, judgment is an act of mind in which particulars are subsumed under general and universal principles. In a deep way, Kant extends the medieval notion of synderesis. He emphasizes the ordering and deciphering possibilities that present themselves to the mind. Like his ancient predecessors, Kant sees judgment in a moral light, that is, connected to ethics.

I would not disagree with these sorting and motivating-toward-action visions of the philosophers. Indeed, judgment is a particular form of thinking or calculating that is simply different than rational computation or even wonder: judgment applies rationality to particular circumstances. What is lacking, however, in traditional accounts is an analysis of that which gives content to judgment—content that is not simply derivative of the imagination or the mind. In particular, I refer to the situation or the world in which the one who is judging is immersed. This situation in which one finds oneself imposes on the mind a need to make a judgment and to act. More importantly, the situation may condition the power of judgment itself. One simply has to look to history to see how historical moments condition and structure our power to judge, much to the chagrin of the philosophers who seek an impermeable and unchanging force of rational judgment. The source of judgment does not solely lie in the power of the mind to render judgment or act in a certain way. Judgment is not only a faculty; rather, it is a response to the weight and exigencies of a situation.

Judgment begins with an accusation or a disturbance directed towards the self that demands a response from the situation and events of the surrounding world of the person. The demand comes from outside our own minds. In our case of living in impasse, for example, the force and pressure of the situation pushes forward into consciousness and in our affective lives an experience in which we feel our self accused of inaction when there should be action—It points out that we are impotent and that we must think otherwise. Judgment calls to us and presents to our minds the distilled sense of reality before us and offers various possibilities of response. After further reflection, many of these possibilities will be dismissed as impossible or irrelevant, but some may be judged to be more possible than others. It is this "more than" that judgment opens—an opening that invites us to begin again, to start over, and attempt a response to the impasse.

What judgment opens is volatile and fragile; it may not be thought through to its fullest extent, or we may not see clearly what is offered by accusations of the outside world that make demands upon us, requiring judgments. Yet it is risk that the opening of judgment offers. We must risk, and when we take the risk and accept its subsequent demands, we face uncertainty. In this sense, action that is motivated by judgment is blind, for the outcome is not predictable.

Hannah Arendt in her *Lectures on Kant's Political Philosophy*[44] argues that judgment is vital for self-becoming. She reads Kant's notion of judgment as laying the ground for a kind of self-testing in which one uses reason to test possibilities that stand before an individual through what Kant calls publicity. Judgment, according to Arendt, is given a unique moral function, as mentioned earlier.[45] It allows us to distinguish good from evil, the beautiful from the ugly. Both Arendt and Kant conceive of judgment as capacity of the autonomous self, a capacity for self-activation. And though this may appear phenomenologically true, impasse reveals another situation. Impasse itself imposes a demand on us, it calls to us. Thinking brings to consciousness what is new about the impasse in which we find ourselves, and judgment is activated in us, generated in us by the pressure of the impasse itself. The self does not merely stand freely and rationally, almost immovably, over a situation, ordering it and deciding what shape it will take. Impasse configures how and what judgment can bring forward. But what comes forward is ordered by judgment as possibilities about which we have to decide what matters for our own being, others, and the world. Judgment gives shapes to possibilities precisely as possibilities: it shows that the situation of impasse has many facets to it, numerous aspects, some or all of which can be thought about, analyzed, and responded to. It is judgment that activates in us the power to *possibilize*, to make things possible or to see reality as a series of possibilities. The seemingly unilateral weight and pressure of impasse enters our inner world, charges our feeling, making us aware of ourselves as a self while also discharging the power of judgment to receive reality not simply as a fact but as constituted by a series of possibilities. Judgment is activated by the demand to examine and choose among possibilities the ways to bear and perhaps think otherwise about the suffering caused by the impasse. It *possibilizes* what the impasse presents to us in our inner life. The "otherwise" of what presents itself as real or as a fact is displaced by the power of judgment to open up possibilities from what is presented by the external situation of impasse.

Willing

If judgment is the response of possibilities to the accusation of inaction or the demand for action that stems from a situation of the outside world, what is willing? Arendt, in *The Life of the Mind*, reminds us that philosophers are very divided on whether or not willing exists. The history of philosophy is marked by hard core determinists who maintain that there is nothing like the freedom of the will, as well as thinkers who argue for a very powerful form of voluntarism. Of course, there are more moderate positions between voluntarism and determinism. The will is generally understood as a power to move or bring about actions that are either called for by judgments, imagination, or thinking. Arendt maintains that the will appears when the mind is confronted with a willy-nilly, *nolo-volo* situation: it is conflicted and cannot decide what to do and so feels that it must do something. This is the force of the will, but it is judgment that enters to help the will move and enact itself. Judgment has the potential to guide the will, especially on matters that must distinguish between good and evil, the beautiful and the ugly. But does the will arise spontaneously when one finds oneself in an impasse, the *nolo-volo* of Arendt?

Not all actions are willed, yet they happen. Will is a particular phenomenon that is born, as Arendt says, of some kind of impasse. But the impasse is not simply grounded in the Platonic impasse of the mind; rather, the impasse, like our contemporary political impasse, is a situation of the world. The full action of the will is launched through the force of judgment, which brings us to the impasse and forces us to think, to imagine otherwise, creating an opening of possibility. The will assents to carry through what judgment has made visible. In this sense, the will is an adjunct power, a kind of impetus or initiative.

The Italian philosopher Luigi Pareyson argues that persons have a unique capacity, namely, initiative, which allows them to singularize and universalize their humanity. *Iniziativa* is a polyvalent word which easily translates to "initiative," understood as the capacity to begin, create, or undertake something (before anyone else), but it also includes the sense of "interdependence," as well as "drive" or "impetus." When Pareyson uses the term to describe what lies at the core of the human person, the sense of force, power, or drive is palpable.

> The unique ground of the person's singularity and universality is initiative. On the one hand, initiative concretizes and therefore singularizes the person. On the other hand, it gives value to and

hence universalizes the person. Initiative is simultaneously an exigency, a decision, and a valuing: decision offers determination to the exigency, thus concretizing and singularizing exigency; valuing locates such a determination within the domain of values, giving the determination its value while universalizing it.[46]

A person's situation—historical, local, and in relation to oneself, others, and God—imposes demands. These demands, in turn, call forward a free, decisive response to the exigencies of the situation. As Pareyson explains:

> The more the person freely shapes and defines its profile, the more its decisions become circumscribed (even if they are never constrained) by the historical concreteness within which the person acquires its own consistency. The process of singularization is a process of election and selection, that is, of originary and progressive qualification in which the person's uniqueness [*irripetibilità*] is increasingly affirmed. Such uniqueness, understood as a determination of initiative, is never a pure quality precisely because it is an axiological determination.[47]

The decisions that flow freely from one's own initiative singularize and concretize the person, giving the person a more defined profile. Yet, and this is where Pareyson's view differs from more traditional French existentialist accounts of the person, decisions produce effects on the situation which, in turn, involve and affect others. Values are given to the situation and the person can be seen as valuing. In the experience of impasse, actions of will, namely, the will to turn inward and think otherwise, may help further singularize the person, opening the oikeiotic becoming at home with oneself, but certain values about oneself, the world, and others also emerge. These values may be negative, in which case they can be potentially destructive. But they may also be positive and affirming. All values have an objective force, that is, they establish certain concrete modes of behavior of affinity or repulsion towards things and people. When we value something, we may care for and love it. These values may motivate us to will certain actions or responses. The pressure of an impasse, and the content of that impasse, for example, the human suffering it causes, may push us to will to care more intensely about others, to help them, and to take care of them. It may also push us to will to think otherwise.

Newness and the Inner Turn

We come now to an important question: If one's interiority, through its thinking, willing, imagining, and judging, can serve as a viable source for *oikeiosis*, understood as a response to impasse, how do these capacities form a self and a new politics? In other words, how can a turn inward assist us in a time of impasse? Does political impasse not trap us within our immanence?

It would be naïve to think that interiority necessarily translates into a complete or absolute response to impasse. Impasses can be so forceful or so overwhelming that a turn inward becomes impossible, that is, no interiority is accessible. For example, Arendt discusses how totalitarian regimes produce in their citizens a kind of impasse that takes over the psyche and eliminates interiority. In her analysis of concentration camps in *The Origins of Totalitarianism*, she admits that the breakdown of the legal concept of the person achieved through the classification of Jews and others as nonpersons was key for the annihilation of millions. She remarks:

> The first essential step on the road to total domination is to kill the juridical person in the human. This was done, on the one hand, by putting certain categories of people outside the protection of the law and enforcing at the same time, through the instrument of denationalization, the non-totalitarian world into recognition of lawlessness; it was done, on the other, by placing the concentration camp outside the normal judicial procedure in which a definite crime entails a predictable penalty.[48]

But Arendt also makes an important point regarding another discourse, namely, morality. For the Nazis to succeed, they needed to break down not only legal concepts but also those concepts inscribed in moral psychology. Arendt argues that the breakdown of the legal concept without a moral breakdown of the person would have given prisoners a chance to hold on to their conscience and the just conviction that they had been unjustly condemned; resistance would have been more possible.

> Totalitarian terror achieved its most terrible triumph when it succeeded in cutting the moral person off from the individualist escape and in making the decisions of conscience absolutely questionable and equivocal. When a man is faced with the alternative of betraying and thus murdering his friends or of sending his wife and children, for whom he is in every sense responsible, to their death; when even suicide would mean the

immediate murder of his own family—how is he to decide? The alternative is no longer between good and evil, but between murder and murder.... Through the creations of conditions under which conscience ceases to be adequate and to do good becomes utterly impossible, the consciously organized complicity of all men in the crimes of totalitarian regimes is extended to the victims and thus made really total.[49]

Arendt recognizes the existence of a moral person who knows how to distinguish right from wrong and who draws value and worth from the decisions he or she makes, decisions that steer the person away from causing unjust harm to others and to the self. From its inception, philosophy has thought about ethics: what is right and what is wrong, what is a just character and an unjust one. Arendt sees Socrates as the thinker who can distinguish between good and evil, and show us why it is better to choose the good and avoid the harm that ensues from choosing evil. This culminates in moral personhood, which she views as critical for the good functioning of any political society. For Arendt, a thinking person may prevent a moral wrong through judgment, thereby blocking the horrendous possibility of repetitive, long-lasting violence and brutality in impasse.

It should also be noted that political impasse, while it produces possible responses within thought, may be so overwhelming that those possibilities remain trapped within the immanence of the human psyche. This does not mean they do not have an impact on the life of the individual that brings them forward in the life of the mind; the ideas and potential responses may continue to nourish the individual, providing hope and making possible constancy.

Moreover, if the ideas are communicated, even though they are not enacted at a given time because of the force of the impasse, they may be taken up in some future time, perhaps as a response to a different problem, crisis, or impasse. The history of ideas is deeply marked by these once abandoned ideas revitalized and expanded in new situations. Walter Benjamin and Jacques Derrida, in their discussions of messianism, ruminate on the power of history to bring forward ideas that may have use or impact in the future: the ideas whose time will come. Arendt believes that a who or somebody may lay down a narrative through speech and/or deed that will impact a society in the future.

There are times when possible responses to political impasse, as manifested within a person's inner life, may be communicated and shared with others bringing forward the ideas that may lead to the destabilizing of an impasse. The idea of separating faith from secular society, for example, articulated in the Peace of Westphalia, gave birth to a new kind of sovereignty and provided potential for a new understanding of politics, religion, and the relation between the two, even though various philosophers, including medieval thinkers like Marsilius of Padova, had already intimated the need to separate political and religious realms. Ideas are not always the property of one individual: they occur within a given historical situation and usually take time to unfold. Each idea is an expression of an interiority that responds to a situation and even launches or calls for some response, decision, or initiative. The idea of a Copernican world, for example, is not exclusive to Copernicus; many had similar notions, including Nicholas of Oresmes, but it was Copernicus, building upon the insights and ideas of others, who articulated more precisely, and supported with mathematical evidence, the possibility of a heliocentric universe. In many ways, he was responding to the impasse created by the conflict of a new and developing science of astronomy that was at odds with a Ptolemaic universe justified with Aristotelian-Scholastic inspired theological claims.

What sustains the turn inward in a time of impasse? What keeps us going? I believe the answer is desire. Arendt, like Augustine, acknowledges that desire or love is part of being human, but whereas Augustine sees desire as always pushing the mind either toward or away from God, who is love and can condition the will and reason, Arendt sees desire as independent and striving for its own objects. But desire or love does not occupy a place within her view of mind. Thinking is not moved by desire, for Arendt, but by Socratic wisdom and *aporia*. Unlike Plato, she never discusses at any great length the erotic aspect of wonder. As we have seen in our earlier discussion, desire can motivate knowing, but not the quest for meaning. (Arendt never completed the section on judging in *The Life of the Mind*, but desire is not mentioned.) The will is distinguished from desire, even transforming it into intention. Augustine, true to his neo-Platonic roots, believes the soul is always moved by desire, including all of its capacities and powers, especially reason and the will, which work with desire and love to pursue their objects. In making the distinction between desire, thinking, judging, and willing, as well as by keeping desire distinct or transforming it into something other, Arendt introduces a significant cleavage into her description of mind. Love or desire does not collaborate in any significant way as they are distinct and powerful, autonomous but related. Why does this matter?

The separation of desire from the faculties of the mind strips these faculties of passion and pleasure, the two fundamental affects of love or desire. Surely, thinking, judging, and willing can produce their own pleasures, but when they are lived out with passion and desire, the pleasures they offer are intensified. They can also cause anguish, as Augustine admits in his *Confessions*. Let us recall his famous call for chastity, which he simultaneously asks to be delayed. I do believe, along with Aristotle and Epicurus, that we are born to experience pleasure and that pleasure is a desired end. Desire can help us achieve that end, especially if it is directed to some good, as both Aristotle and Augustine maintain. It would also be remiss not to mention that desire can produce suffering when unfulfilled or disappointed, as when a love turns sour. Augustine believed the orientation of desire to the right objects, through God's grace, could help one intensify the pleasure of reason and willing: "Hence the mind is fed by the source of joy."[50] Augustine's conversion to God reorients his whole being and world—his *Confessions* are full of delightful and heart-filled praise for what God has accomplished in him.

One of the great perils of correlating love and desire with the faculties of the mind is that desire may thwart the activities of the mind, but, according to both Augustine and Arendt, this is part of human fallibility. One can also grow in love, according to Augustine, as social relations between humans and God and those between humans and others can become more robust if one commits oneself to the desire or love for God. Thinking, willing, and judging, from the moment they appear to us in consciousness as possibilities, have their own motivating structure: one thought will call forward another thought, and this produces a certain affect in us: we desire to know more, to think more, to will and judge more and correctly. These faculties of the life of the mind have their own animating force that comes to be lived as a desire to continue to think, judge, and will.

In her discussion of motivation, Edith Stein argues that a form of intuitive belief presents itself in motivated acts pushed by the life of spirit and the force of life itself. Belief pushes the individual forward to act; it is a kind of motivating desire that is not reducible to actions produced by psychic causality and/or rationality. Motivating acts, such as thinking and willing, can push the individual further to desire to undertake further actions.

Motivation, Stein argues, is a unique act of consciousness that is deeply connected to the life of psyche but also to the life of spirit, the realm of reason, and free will. The connection of conscious acts that constitute themselves as motivated are understood as one act emerging out of another. Furthermore, the full achievement or fulfillment of their sense, such that they can be understood properly as motivated acts, lies in the grasping that one act leads to the other wherein the latter act emerges out of the former, and the former act executes itself for the sake of the other. Stein writes:

> Motivation, in our general sense, is the connection that acts get into with one another: not a mere blending like that of simultaneously or sequentially ebbing phases of experiences, or the associative tying together of experiences, but an emerging of the one out of the other, a self-fulfilling or being fulfilled of the one on the basis of the other for the sake of the other. The structure of experiences, which can enter into relationships of motivation all by themselves, is decisive throughout for the essence of those

relations.... Every explicit motivation essentially devolves into an implicit one after its execution, and you can essentially explicate every implicit motivation—for example, the motivation included within faith in an unproved, "intuitively" anticipated theorem. In the different spheres of intentional experience, one or the other kind of motivation prevails at any given time. In the area of simple perception we're mostly dealing with implicit motivation.[51]

Remarkable in her account of motivation is the claim that when we experience it, we grasp its sense (*Sinn*) in a specific epistemological mode, not as a form of psychic causality (i.e., not as an if→then or "as if" relation), and not as a rational or logical deduction as in a categorial synthesis in which all terms are explicitly manifest, but as a kind of induction that is seized as a belief. Stein speaks here of faith, which is akin to the perceptual faith that accompanies most of our natural experience, especially bodily habits. For example, as Maurice Merleau-Ponty notes, when we reach for a door handle, the hand automatically anticipates the form of the handle before we even touch it. We believe the handle requires a certain bodily movement before we actually feel the handle.

Whereas acts of free will are marked by a spontaneous and actively conscious decision of the I (*Ich kann*), motivated acts can be marked by both explicit and implicit belief. Stein observes:

It can come to pass explicitly, but it can also be present only implicitly. It's a case of an explicit motivation, for example, if we have a flash of insight and believe in connection with an inference from the premises to the conclusion. On the other hand, if we carry out a mathematical proof and use a theorem that we had insight into at some earlier time on the basis of its postulates but now don't prove anew, then the faith in this theorem is motivated faith, but the motivation is not currently coming to pass. Rather, it's implicit in the concrete act through which the theorem stands before us as a unit and in the determinate mode of believing. Every explicit motivation essentially devolves into an implicit one after its execution, and you can essentially explicate every implicit motivation—for example, the motivation included within faith in an unproved, "intuitively" anticipated theorem. In the different spheres of intentional experience, one or the other kind of motivation prevails at any given time. In the area of simple perception we're mostly dealing with implicit motivation.[52]

We can have an immediate, explicit insight, Stein says, that can directly and consciously motivate or engender another act. Likewise, we may apply a theorem we have learned in the past to a present problem, and though the theorem is no longer present, it is activated because it implicitly motivates an act in the present. In motivated acts, whether explicit or implicit, the ego serves as the go-between.[53]

Motivation, understood as a form of connection between acts, properly belongs, Stein claims, to the spiritual, personal realm, though it is thoroughly enmeshed or intertwined with the psychic and bodily realms also constituent of the human person. It should be remarked here that one of the defining features of Stein's conception of personhood is the profound, lived experience of a personal unity or unified working together of three distinct but related realms of human being, namely, body, psyche, and spirit. In her first work on empathy,

Stein identifies motivation as the vital bridge that makes manifest the intimate connection of these three realms.

If we correlate the faculties of mind with motivating desire, we can have more intense experiences of the life of the mind as it lives itself out, especially in an impasse. Furthermore, such intensity of pleasure and delight can also induce us to lead a life of the mind, encouraging us to think, will, and judge, all of which can lead to a better existence, alone and together. I read Arendt's *The Life of the Mind* as a description of the mind's faculties and our need for their help in making moral decisions to avert evil, as we are told at the beginning of the book, but I also believe Arendt wishes us to experience the kind of life that is fruitful and open to those who embrace the life of the mind. To attach desire and love to the life of the mind enhances and intensifies life, extending it beyond the exercise of the faculties of thinking, judging, and willing. Let us not forget Socrates's delight in the mania that descends on the lover as the lover pursues the form of love. Think of the descriptions of mania that one finds in the *Phaedrus* and the *Ion*: Socrates recognizes the place of mania in the structure of *eros*, even though he is critical of its remaining an end in itself, as it can never then lead to self-disclosure. The *Phaedrus* shows that, in the ascent to an understanding of *eros*, one must go through the mania of desire, but never rest there. There is pleasure in the mania as highlighted in both the *Symposium* and the *Phaedrus*; indeed, this is the critique of Ion the rhapsode: he loses himself in his imitation of Homer. *Eros*, the driving love that motivates us to pursue philosophy, works in conjunction with the dialectic and with Socrates's tireless questioning and indefatigable stinging. He desires it and uses the faculties of the soul to achieve it. Arendt, though admiring of Socrates, strips him of his desire, privileging the object of his search—wisdom—but not paying enough attention to the engine that drives his thought, an engine which is constituent of wisdom itself—love and desire.

The fact is that the life of the mind Arendt describes is marked by a powerful capacity to receive, to be impressed on, and to bear: it is receptive and can be affected by the world, the self, and others. For things to appear in thinking, for example, the mind must receive. The thought-things of thinking, judgments, and willed acts are not creations *ex nihilo*; rather, they need to be affected by things and realities, even ourselves. Desire and love can emerge as responses, both conscious and unconscious, to that which strikes the mind. Stein, for example, wonderfully notes in her Münster lectures[54] on philosophical anthropology that intentionality is a two-way street: we may intend objects of consciousness to understand what things are, but things also intend us—they capture our intention and impress themselves on us. The reaction they produce in us could be understood in terms of desire: they elicit us; they make us desirous to think them through, judge them, and to act or not to act on them through will or nonwill. Joseph Torchia reminds us that Augustine does not view concupiscence in exclusively negative terms for it can also turn our attention and desire to useful and enjoyable things that originate in the outside world, and this consideration helps us acquire knowledge and contemplate the world, the self, others, and God. Torchia argues that Augustine is more worried about idle curiosity, understood as the desire for superfluous knowledge.[55]

The activity that Arendt ascribes to the mind cannot be complete unless we also admit a kind of passivity or receptivity to the mind, which becomes desirous once affected by that which is not reducible to our own interiorities: self, others, and world. The activation of the mind stems, in part, not only from its own energy but also from its being elicited or solicited by desire—the mind needs to be seduced by a desire that emanates from external objects and the world. Perhaps, then, we can read desire, as does Michel Henry, as a passivity that can help awaken our being and mind to live.[56] If we admit the motivating or erotic force of desire as Augustine develops it, namely, the desire to know and think as well as the desire to know who one is in relation to others (the positive sense of *concupiscentia* versus *curiositas*), desire can be seen to have an important place in the life of the mind. And a desire that may be engendered through an inward turn into the life of the mind may help spur on the oikeiotic process that marks a possibility of becoming and thinking otherwise in the time of impasse.

Communifying Possibility and Hope

So far, I have argued that the force of the political situation we call impasse exerts pressure upon individuals, pushing them to think otherwise and activate the power of the life of the mind to formulate a possible response to the impasse. We must recall that the response may be overwhelmingly negative: we may feel completely impotent and unable to do anything except feel stuck in the impasse. But when we do formulate possibilities, how are we to interpret them? Furthermore, can we mine these possibilities to create a stronger, more potent response, understood in the full sense of a communal response? I believe we can.

I call the emergence of a possibility that may have meaningful consequences and/or bring about a desired change or action "hope." I do not wish to launch into a full discussion on the forms or modal possibilities of hope as this would take us away from the matter at hand; rather, I wish to focus on a particular sense of it. Hope is a specific form of possibility that manifests three essential elements that constitute its very being. First, the possibility that emerges with hope is an opening or a response to a situation of seeming impasse: it is conditioned by the closedness or no-exit feeling engendered by a certain situation, such as the political impasse that a group of people feel today, especially in the West. Second, hope has an affective structure: it can lessen anxiety and the feelings of confinement and helplessness inherent in an impasse. With hope, one feels a lifting of the strictures imposed upon the soul. Finally, hope has an existential dimension in that it can reorient our being in the world toward a future. Time is opened up and is no longer experienced as fleeting, closing down, or as simply extending or protracting the moment of impasse.

And though hope is experienced most intimately within our inner lives, as individuated inner lives, it can be communicated to and shared with others. Impasse need not be solitary. Justus Lipsius shared his ideas with friends and consolers and, together in dialogue, they worked out and extended the hope of specific individuals, thereby expanding hope into a genuine communal possibility. Conversation and dialogue, lived in community, are key to the growth of hope. The opening presented to one person must enter the public sphere and be tested and worked upon by those suffering the same political impasse. In *The Human Condition*, Arendt observes that we do not narrate our own stories; instead, others tell our stories and, in so doing, they create a public sphere in which lives are lived as individuals and as communities. In this public sphere, we find common interest rooted in the being that is between individuals, what Arendt calls the *interesse* or the being-between. Words, speaking, and conversations, can all open a shared public space between individuals. Hope, as a form of possibility that marks a thinking otherwise in or a response to a political impasse, can be shared and collectivized, and it is here that one finds hope suddenly becoming a powerful and vivifying possibility that is capable of instigating change, namely, the undoing of the impasse.

Bergson reminds us that certain psychological experiences dilate and completely flood our consciousness. These intense states (and hope can be experienced as an intense inner state) can be communal. Edith Stein speaks of these shared internal states as an *ineindergreifen*, in which we seize the inner life of another person to such a degree that we experience what she calls the solidarity of community.

Stein uses the word *Gemeinschaftserlebnis*, or "lived experience of community," to describe the specific, conscious, lived experience that typifies the essence of community. She starts her analysis by emphasizing community is always lived through the pure I. It is the pure I that experiences solidarity with others. It is wondrous, she declares, how the individual, pure I can enter a community of life with other subjects.[57] The individual, according to Stein, can experience life within what she calls a "super-individual subject."[58] Using the famous example of the death of the troop leader,[59] she describes what she means by the convergence of the individual and the super-individual within the lived experience of community. Recall that this text was written after the First World War, which Stein saw firsthand as a nurse on the front lines, and as a result of which she lost many friends and colleagues. So, she asks the reader to imagine a troop whose much-loved leader perishes. She observes that an individual certainly feels the sadness of the loss; this is one's own personal grief. But she goes on to say that individuals can also feel the collective grief of the community. One feels a communal sadness and, insofar as one does this, he or she lives an experience of solidarity that consists of the communal sadness of the group:

> Certainly I, the individual ego, am filled up with grief. But I feel myself to be not alone with it. Rather, I feel it as *our* grief. The experience is essentially colored by the fact that others are taking part in it, or even more, by the fact that I take part in it only as a member of a community. *We* are affected by the loss, and *we* grieve over it. And this "we" embraces not only all those who feel the grief as I do, but all those who are included in the unity of the group: even the ones who perhaps do not know of the event, and even the members of the group who lived earlier or will live later. We, the we who feel the grief, do it in the name of the total group and of all who belong to it. We feel this subject affected within ourselves when we have an experience of community. I grieve as a member of the unit, and the unit grieves within me.[60]

I am simultaneously conscious of my own grief and that of the group of my fellow troop members. In this way, Stein says, the I has an individual as well as a superindividual experience. Notice that the I is never absorbed into the superindividual experience, but experiences both simultaneously.

As a lived experience of community is lived (*erlebt*), Stein observes, it can acquire greater color and depth and even grow in significance, especially if it endures; it grows in the continuity of its living.[61] There can be many variations within the living of the lived community experience, but these always take place within the unity of its "fulfilled" sense[62] and its meaning-context:

> But only in the experience of the one who feels the "appropriate" grief is the intention which runs throughout the collective experience of community fulfilled and satisfied. It must be stressed that besides the purely objective intention, an intention toward the communal experience is inherent within the experiences that are directed toward a super-individual object—inasmuch as that object stands before us as super-individual—and that our experience is constitutive for that object. We feel the grief as something belonging to the unit, and through this grief we are calling for the grief of the unit to be realized.[63]

And if there is no continuity or duration of sense within the unified experience of solidarity, the lived experience can fade away. Likewise, if the troop members do not feel a communal sadness at the loss of their leader, there is no communal lived experience. Furthermore, it should be remarked that, though the lived experience of community is typified by one living in the experience of the other in solidarity, the sense of solidarity can arise and grow with a myriad of experiences in many forms with many intentional objects. Stein uses the example of the troop's sadness, but many other experiences, including those of love, joy, or boredom, can serve as a communal sense around which one lives the experience of community. Finally, the lived experience of community can be felt with varying intensities; all members experiencing solidarity in relation to a specific intentional object do not experience it identically. Stein notes that the lived experience of community is filtered and lived through individual personalities; it can be felt passionately, superficially, persistently, or even fleetingly. What is seized is the sense of solidarity that characterizes the lived community experience and, therefore, one lives within the other in an experience of community.

Stein concludes her analysis by reaffirming that superindividual experience occurs within the consciousness of individuals. There is no super-consciousness or flow of lived consciousness outside individuals. One lives the experience of the other in solidarity with the other, but one never loses one's individuality; there is no communal pure I. There are only individual pure *I*s that direct consciousness toward the superindividual experience of community.

Stein sees phenomenology and philosophy as offering the individual the opportunity to reflect upon its own existence, understood in the broadest sense possible, that is uniquely its own. The immanent sphere of ownness (*Eigenheitssphäre*) that phenomenology claims to uncover through an investigation of individual, conscious experience is unique and foundational, more so than the fields, results, and objects of inquiry that belong to the empirical sciences. This sphere of ownness is the locus of *oikeiosis*. It is a realm that also admits communal possibilities that ultimately render the impasse not merely a solitary field of experience, but also a realm of potential plurality and intersubjectivity.

The Experience of the Initial Possibility of Freedom

A self that experiences the hope of possibility while in political impasse also experiences freedom from within and from without, from inside and outside. Isaiah Berlin tells us that freedom can be experienced positively, as the ability to do something, or negatively, as when one's freedom is inhibited by certain opposing forces or societal laws. A situation or state of affairs allows certain freedoms that enable a person to live or carry out certain acts, thoughts, and feelings. Gerda Walther notes that one of the very first and intimate forms of freedom occurs within the life of the ego's sphere. In phenomenology, when one brackets one's natural attitude and one assumes the phenomenological stance, one becomes aware of one's own consciousness and a zero point of orientation, or a pure I, around which consciousness appears to move. The I can consciously see a foreground and a background; to borrow Husserl's language, there is a horizon of consciousness. This consciousness also has specific content and the I can pause to examine the content in order to try and understand what is presenting itself to consciousness. Fascinating for Walther is the fact that the I can select which content it will focus on while it ignores other content. This power or capacity to select content, to direct consciousness from the zero point of orientation, is the manifestation of freedom "*Keim der Freiheit*."[64]

But freedom is also an experience that arises spontaneously from within us, as Bergson rightfully and powerfully reminds us in his writings. It is this latter form of freedom that accompanies the enlivening activity of hope. The self made manifest in the affect of impasse, as it begins to think otherwise and formulate possible responses to the impasse, recognizes that it is also free; the spontaneous product of thinking otherwise, understood as a possibility to be otherwise, simultaneously generates in its very appearing the freedom, albeit only in its initial stages, an initiating possibility rooted in the horizon that the thinking and being otherwise bring forward in and through its content. We see this concretized with the birth of new ideas or the creation of original works of art or the imagination. Freedom also arises, however, in the very beginning and actualization of the execution of the response, either individual or shared, to the force of political impasse. Freedom is not the condition for the possibility of action: it arises with action and is born in action—the action of thinking otherwise or the action of responding to the impasse, collectively and individually. This freedom grows and intensifies, just as our response can grow and intensify. The inner experience of freedom parallels the vivifying awareness that we ourselves can think otherwise, that the impasse is only temporary and not eternal.

Dilating the Time of Impasse from Within

The relation of oneself to oneself, achieved through an inward turn brought on by the pressure of impasse, also has the possibility of reconfiguring one's lived experience of time by dilating it from within.[65] Time can be opened and extended in the impasse as one can live its moments intensely. The Italian philosopher Ugo Perone maintains, following Heidegger, that the relation to our own being reveals that this relation is certainly one of care framed within temporality, but it is also an intense relation of lingering within intensified moments of time. Indubitably, the oikeiotic process described above opens up the relation of the self to being. But I also think there is more that can be added to this relation between oneself and time. There may even be a sense of security in one's own being, as it is given from moment to moment, as Stein affirms. In the end, perhaps impasse can reframe our relation to our being, to temporality, and to the sense of ourselves, not as transient but as being constantly given new moments of being, new moments of hope. Impasse may make this visible to us.

Martin Heidegger's *Being and Time* revolutionized the twentieth century's way of thinking about time and its relation to being. His careful analysis of care and temporality exposes a new fundamental way of being for *Dasein* as it questions its being in the world. Heidegger's insights had a deep and meaningful impact on the thinking of Stein, but also on the Italian philosopher Ugo Perone. In his work *The Possible Present*,[66] Perone argues for a conception of the present, always occurring within the dynamic of the flow of and within the "ecstases" of time, that facilitates the very possibility of lingering in being and thought. Stein, especially in her magnum opus, *Finite and Eternal Being*,[67] argues that the flow of time reveals that the living present is experienced as being-held-in-being, a security of being that arises from the expectation that being will continue to be given to us as one moment passes into the next.

Lingering and security, then, are the two fundamental comportments toward being revealed by both Stein's and Perone's analyses of the present. While their conclusions about time are both valid, I wish to argue for the possibility of an intimate relation between lingering and security that may lay the ground for a new lived experience of time in the impasse. Lingering requires a deep ontic sense of security in order for it to manifest itself, but lingering, in turn, conditions the intensity with which we feel the very security offered to us by being. In short, a dialectical relation between lingering and security comes to exist: while the security in being is a fundamental condition for the possibility of the manifestation of lingering, it is lingering in being that can intensify the quality and very lived experience of security, and give rise to a more meaningful relation of one's own being to itself, others, and the world in the lived present, ultimately creating intense temporal moments in which one can meaningfully and creatively think otherwise in a time of impasse. One of the major complaints about contemporary life is a lack of time: people are always busy and there is never enough time to do what they feel, need, or want to do. In impasse, though, time seems to have come to a standstill, either through the sense of nonmovement or lack of change, or through the repetition of what seem to be the same cycle of events. The dilation of inner time creates an experience in which one can rethink the relation of oneself to one's situation, the world, and others.

The Possible Present: A Threshold

In his deeply insightful work, *The Possible Present*, Ugo Perone argues that time is experienced in two unique ways. First, there is physical time, the time of nature, which moves forward chronologically. This time can be measured or anticipated in three primary modes: the past, the present, and the future. This is the time of the sciences: one can measure a heart rate per second, for example, or time a race. Second, drawing from Husserl and Heidegger as well as Bergson, there is the time we live, replete with meanings, a time that flows with its own rhythms and cadences. It is the time of what phenomenology calls lived experience (*Erlebnis*) or inner time consciousness. Here, the emphasis is on how time is lived, for us, in conscious experience. Rather than measurements of instants of the past, present, and future, we have, Husserl teaches us, retention of the past or having been, the living present of the now, and anticipation or expectation of a future. Heidegger phenomenologically recasts temporality as the deep structure of care, which reveals how Dasein's being unfolds in the world.

Drawing from but also distancing himself from Heidegger, Perone argues that Heidegger's predilection for the future or anticipatory structure of lived time is problematic.

> Heidegger's attempt goes in the direction of rooting temporality in the finitude of Dasein. To avoid all risks of ontological essentialization, he chooses the primacy of the purely anticipatory modality of the future. *Zeitlichkeit zeitig sich ursprünglich aus der Zukunft*: Temporality temporalizes itself primordially out of the future. The consequence is that in order to escape the inauthentic temporality of the now, which is reflected in the ontology of *Vorhandenheit*, one consigns oneself to the primacy of the not-yet, of the instant [*Augenblick*] as manifestation of the time that passes [*vergeht*].
>
> (PP 9)

In describing time as passing instants, Heidegger maintains that it is impossible to authentically seize what it is for Dasein to be, for it has no access to that which has passed. Dasein inauthentically tries to make present that which is impossibly so. Dasein can anticipate a future, but this future is not-yet. In the temporality of the instants of the past, present, and future, there is a nothing: the nothing of the having been of the past, the nothing of the fleeting instant of the present, and the nothing of the not-yet of the future. This nothing reveals Dasein as profoundly finite, incapable of transcending the time to which it is subject. Perone notes:

> The extreme attempt at situating oneself on the side of finite temporality is accompanied by the anticipating consummation of time. In this context Dasein itself appears as inexorably inclined toward the direction of the not, so much so that it can find its authenticity only through the anticipation of non-being, that is, of death. What emerges is a temporality inexorably attracted toward the ending of finitude, and unable to grasp the initialness [*inizialità*] of time. What also derives is a life that is thought within the transcendental horizon of death and an ontology that is marked by an immanent nihilistic outcome.
>
> (PP 10)

Heidegger's failure to account for the initialness of time, so Perone claims, serves as the launching pad for Perone's own discussion of the present, understood as a possible present and as a threshold. Perone admits, however, that Heidegger lays down an important challenge: how can we not reduce the present to presence, a presence that can never fully be, a presence that traditionally philosophy has sought to make clear and distinct (PP 14). Perone notes that we must reconceive the present outside of traditional philosophical categories, including the eternal, the instant, and the now (PP 10). If the present is eternal, no extension of time is possible, nor are any discrete moments in time. If time is eternal, how and why do we come to experience the loss or passing of time? Furthermore, if the present is simply a now that can supposedly be shared in common with other subjects, the problem arises of how to account for the unique, individual experience of subjective time outside of this communal now. Finally, if the present is understood simply to be an instant, though the instant may account for the loss or passing of time or its fall into nothingness, the category of the instant cannot account, by definition, for its integration into the flow of time in general, that is the becoming of another instant that somehow is connected and follows from the previous instant.

For Perone, the present is a beginning in the sense that it is a kind of "discriminating" limit that divides it from two other modes of the human experience (that is, past and future) of time and natural temporality in general.

> The present is that which discriminates, the passing that withholds, the hand that closes up so as to support itself and others.... Such a divide can be so short, unexpected, and extraneous that it holds only for an instant, which is nevertheless decisive because it divides time and ploughs through history by virtue of interruptions. [The divide] also designs the now to which we belong reciprocally and that crosses shared paths with us. Somehow [the divide] can also be the eternal, and it can constitute an image of it in its having secured forever something that could no longer be and that was drawn to being and saved through it.

(PP 14–15)

The divide is then described as an existence (PP 15). In the lived experience of the flow of time, a present begins: it surges against and is consciously and meaningfully differentiated from a past and a future. The present is not constituted simply as a Bergsonian duration or intensity, but as divisionary beginning. Yet, we do not possess this beginning, for it can never be made present in the form of a presentification or eternalization. The implication for the present of the impasse is that it is already divided, which is an important recognition for us to be able to move in the impasse. Perone observes:

> Time is essentially and originally that which I do not have. Such not-having that traces and marks me is nevertheless the unbalance on which I build my life daily. The present is the threshold where the not-having of time (subjective genitive) intersects existence. It is the fleeting intersecting of an encounter. Life is always the recommencing attempt at expanding such a small opening and controlling time by seconding it without merely suffering from its offenses. All this, in truth, eliminates presence, because in the form of objectification presence confronts one with the contradictoriness of having and not-having. Here having is instead a seconding, where activity and passivity are equally legitimized, and moreover, where the subject of having is from the beginning confronted with the alterity of something that escapes not because it is other (intolerable positivism or transcendence). Rather, [the subject is] confronted with the alterity of a time that is essentially fleetingness and that therefore confronts the subject with alterity (from which it would nevertheless like to protect itself).
>
> (PP 15)

The subject who lives the threshold in the impasse is confronted with a having and not-having of time. The not-having given by the fleeting of time reveals an alterity that is not the subject, a not-me. And it is this experience of the not-me that makes visible or felt the presence of a subjectivity, one who undergoes and lives the threshold experience of the possible present. The threshold is a horizon, a limit that opens and closes a space in which the subject is given to itself, but not fully. The limit of the threshold also manifests that which is not the subject.[68] The threshold of the present is truly a possibility in the sense that it stands between having and not-having, being and not-being. It lies within the freedom and the power of the subject to dilate the possible present in order to help build a world as well as a narrative account and interpretations of oneself and the world in which one dwells. The possibility of the present is a beginning but also an initiative. This double sense of the *inizialità*, understood as both beginning and subjective initiative, stems from the work of Ugo Perone's teacher, Luigi Pareyson, who sees in persons a unique capacity for initiative that helps build a world and personhood, but also helps build an ethics of responsibility.[69] Impasse can be marked by this sense of initiative.

Perone claims the threshold that is the present manifests certain features. He notes that we must not think of the threshold as a line; rather, it is a zone (PP 16)—a zone in the impasse. Furthermore, "this zone can be recognized only *a posteriori*, insofar as one has crossed it or has anticipated its crossing in the form of imagination. Also, it cannot be inhabited, but only crossed over. Finally, the one who perceives the threshold simultaneously dilates and deepens it" (PP 16). Drawing on the work of Walter Benjamin, Perone describes the threshold as a space of co-presencing that is both familiar and disquieting (PP 16). The threshold of the present is marked by fleetingness where one is present, but never fully so. The present is never fully my own: "In this sense and from this perspective, despite the spatial origin of the metaphor, [the threshold] seems capable of expressing an essential element of time: its structural feature of fleetingness, its essential never-being-mine, and the cipher of negativity that belongs to it" (PP 17). Perone follows Heidegger, affirming a negation that manifests itself in the experience of the present, but he also wishes to affirm the present's presencing: the present manifests content.

If the present of the impasse is fleeting reality and it is not mine, it then belongs to no one. It is only for "someone" (PP 17), but for no one particular, individual person.

> The threshold is the not-mine that nevertheless is for me. It is the place and time of the crossing; the path that is proposed to me, the memory of what has been crossed, the waiting for a pass. It is not, however, the place of dwelling. The threshold turns [things] upside down because it transforms the over-here into an over-there, the inside into the outside, and the mine into the other's. It affects the I that crosses it, which becomes alienated. The threshold installs itself in the I, and not the I in the threshold. The time that the I covers, indeed, traverses the I, and turns it upside down.
>
> (PP 17)

For Perone, the present is never fully present; it is not a Bergsonian intensity or *élan* or duration, nor is it simply fleeting and ungraspable: it is an in-between. From a phenomenological perspective, he claims that presencing, retention, and anticipation are all moments of the present, a position that is in line with most readings of Husserlian phenomenology. Memory can retain aspects of the present, while anticipating an opening of time through the dilation of time by the subject:

> The threshold that has been overcome is not eliminated; rather, it is withheld in memory. The threshold is even the protrusion of the memory of that to which we no longer belong. The threshold is severe because it destabilizes; it is severe because it never lets one go. It protrudes into the I, who thought itself able to dominate it, and brings to the I the not-having-time, which is the time that one has in the present.
>
> (PP 18)

What is unique about Perone's discussion of the threshold, especially as it connects to the sense of impasse being developed here, is the positioning of the subject and affectivity. The threshold has a deep and marking structure, which shapes the life of the subject, but also allows the subject to dilate the present in order to create a world and a sense of self, both of which are seized in retrospective apprehension.[70] It should come as no surprise that Perone places an emphasis on both subjectivity and affectivity as these two themes are highly privileged in his work.[71] In a deep sense, time gives the I to itself, but it is not the I of identity, the ego of modern philosophy. What is given is a sense of selfhood, of appropriation: if the threshold is a beginning marked by possibility, a subject is a possibility that can come to be here within this space. By dilating and even compressing the present in the impasse, a subject opens up senses of itself, senses that mark the life of a subject, an individual who bears the affects of the time of the present. The subject can linger in the present, thereby experientially lengthening it.[72] For Perone, the present becomes a remainder that cannot be taken away from us.[73]

The Time of Being-Held in Being and the Giving of Time

Undoubtedly, both Ugo Perone and Edith Stein would agree with Heidegger that the present is both fleeting and, therefore, negating. But whereas Perone views the present as a possible beginning in which the finite subject feels itself and comes to be, Stein views the present as something given, and not of our own making: the present is a becoming of being, which calls us to fuller personhood, both human and divine. In *Finite and Eternal Being*, Stein argues, as do Descartes and Husserl, that one of the most evident things we can say about ourselves is that we exist (FEB 35–36). But our existence is also most certainly marked by a passing. What is flows away into nonexistence. We live our lives between these two poles of existing and not existing. The move from being to nonbeing is a change and it marks the flow of time. Stein notes:

> When I turn toward being as it is in itself, it reveals to me a dual aspect: that of being and that of not-being. The "I am" is unable to endure this dual perspective: that in which "I am" is subject to change, and since being and the intellectual movement ("in which" I am) are not separated, this being is likewise subject to change. The "former" state of being is past and has given way to the present

state of being. This means that the being of which I am conscious as mine is inseparable from temporality. As actual being... [i]t is a "now" in between a "no longer" and a "not yet."

(FEB 37)

If there is a movement or change from being to nonbeing, for Stein, following Aristotle and Thomas Aquinas, we must also posit both possible being and actual being, potency and act, *dynamis* and *energeia*. Being itself and its changes and movements enclose within themselves a potential to be that can actualize itself; this actualization passes into nonbeing, which signifies the completion or finite end of an act of being as it moves into nonbeing (FEB 1–2, 31–34).

Both Perone and Stein recognize the potential in being and both understand the position of the lived past in relation to the past and the future, but it is the experience of the present that is somewhat different for each philosopher, especially as they respond to what they see as Heidegger's privileging of the future and his critique of traditional philosophy's emphasis on full presencing of the present. For Stein, the present is not a threshold experience marked by both dilation and rupture; rather, she argues that the present is an experience of unification and radical alterity. The present is phenomenologically described as manifesting three unique aspects: becoming, the being of pure I or ego-subject, and a radical Other, who Stein calls God. How do these aspects come to affect the experience of the present of the impasse?

How does Stein account for becoming? What is it? While it is true that we experience ourselves as both being and not being, we also experience ourselves as perduring or persisting through time: time moves relative to our own being. Citing *Die Zeit*, the work of her fellow phenomenologist Hedwig Conrad Martius,[74] Stein writes about the ontic birth of time, a birth that happens in the present. It is true that time conditions being, especially as we exist in time, but time is also transformed as it comes into contact with being. Stein observes, "The peculiar nature of enduring being cannot be understood from the point of view of time, but rather, conversely, time must be understood from the point of view of nondimensional actuality. The 'ontic birth of time' takes place 'in the fully actualized present,' in that actual existence... which establishes a contact with being... at only one point," as something which is given and which in its "givenness is simultaneously something privative": a "being suspended between not-being and being" (FEB 40).

Though one is in-between being and not-being, which is like Perone's threshold, Stein posits an enduring or becoming that is an "actual existence," that is, one lives an enduring point that actually exists. Perone emphasizes a real fleeting of being, whereas Stein sees becoming as an actual state that is marked by a kind of enduring being. But here we meet with a great difficulty: If temporal being always immediately passes over into nonbeing, and if thus nothing that is past can "stand firm and remain," is it then not meaningless to speak of enduring units? How can we arrive at a unit that extends beyond the fleeting moment? The life of the ego thus appears to be nothing but a continuous living-from-the-past-into-the-future whereby the potential is constantly actualized and the actual constantly sinks back into potentiality, which affects the possibility of the threshold of the impasse discussed above. Or, to express it differently: that which is not fully alive reaches the height of its vitality, and that which is now fully alive becomes a moment later "life that has been lived" (FEB 44). If time is a flow, it admits becoming. To view time as constituted by three moments or ecstases, to borrow Heidegger's terminology, is to misunderstand the unfolding of time. Stein maintains that instants of time like "now," "past," and "future" see time only from the perspective of the completion of time accomplished as opposed to time unfolding. She ascribes to each of the modes of time a durational quality: the past has duration, as do the present and the future. Stein writes:

> To be sure, we constantly take it for granted that there are such enduring units. And, moreover, by "present" we mean not only the fulfilment of the present moment, nor do we mean by "past" and "future" only what precedes and follows this moment within the circumference of an enduring experiential unit, but we must also call present, past, and future such individual enduring units as are experienced in acts of deliberation, of fear, or of joy. We then designate as past an experiential unit which in its entirety has "moved into the past" and thus is no longer organically and structurally active; we designate as future an experiential unit which has not yet reached the height of the present [*Gegenwartshöhe*]; and we call present an experiential unit which, though not fully alive in its entire extension, is engaged in a vital process of becoming and is at every moment in vital contact with the fullness of life.
>
> (FEB 44)

Stein here introduces a Bergsonian perspective on the psychological experience of becoming as a kind of duration whose constitutive moments or aspects are not necessarily distinct, even though one experiences the flow of becoming. Perone's threshold bifurcates being and not-being and situates becoming within them. Stein sees becoming happening within the past, present, and future, which ultimately means that possibility, being, and nothing also become and admit duration. She gives the example of joy. The lived and actual experience of joy moves, and as it moves it becomes past, present, and can even anticipate future moments of joy (FEB 45, 47). Whereas Perone's threshold divides, Stein's present is one of becoming: it is marked by the unity and connectedness of the flow of content or experience as they alter in time.

Though lived experience and being admits of durational becoming, it still requires being for it to manifest as the distinct and clear experience of being truly or really present, past, or future. Some parts of the whole of a becoming must attain fullness of being in order for the experience of being to keep moving into nonbeing and to keep moving *tout court*; otherwise, we lapse into an eternal present devoid of the flow of time. As Stein observes, "owing to the fact that one or another part of such a unit steadily—though only for a brief moment—reaches the height of being, the whole unit receives a share in being and reveals itself as actually present, i.e., as something actual" (FEB 46). In short, human beings experience being and their being, in particular, as a whole becoming, whose constituent parts move in units of greater or lesser intensity as they become more distinct from one another. As it moves through time, being admits duration. Duration means that parts of being are becoming past, present, and future while other parts are fully or actually past, present, or future. Stein has introduced a unifying durational becoming into the classical concept of constituent instants of time. The implication for the inner experience of time of the impasse is clear: the dilating moment of becoming has within itself real moments of being that perdure, that are kept in being, and so thinking and relating to one's being otherwise can unfold in such moments of being in becoming. The cycles of repetition of the nonprogression of time that typify the experience of impasse can now admit a sense of becoming that also contains real moments of being, with lingering content and meaningful possibility.

We come now to the second aspect of Stein's understanding of the present. Perone argues that the threshold demands a subject. For Stein, the subject, understood in Husserl's sense as the pure ego, is given: it accompanies all experience of being and has a unique being that is its own; it has a life.

> This ego is alive, and its life is its *being*. It lives perhaps right now in the experience of joy, a little while later in longing, and again a little later in thoughtful reflection, but most of the time in several such experiential units simultaneously. But while joy fades away, longing dies, and reflection ceases, the ego does not fade or pass away: It is alive in every now. This does not mean, however, that it possesses eternal life.
>
> (FEB 48)

For Perone, the subject has the potential and the initiative to dilate the present, whereas, for Stein, the durational present requires the life of the ego in order for it to have being. The ego stands in a relation to its own being and the being that it experiences:

> The fact that the experiential contents attain to real being, although they touch it only punctually [*punktuell*] at any given moment, may now appear a little less enigmatic. The real being

they touch is in fact not *their* being, since in and of themselves they are incapable of real being. The experiential contents receive a share in respect to what owes its being to the ego and rises to the level of being by virtue of and within the ego, the latter thus exists in a preeminent sense. The ego is not, to be sure, *existentially superior* in the sense that it could be said to embody the *height of being* (as compared with *rudimentary degrees of being*) but rather in a sense that indicates a relationship existing between a *carrier* and the *thing carried*....

(FEB 49)

The ego-subject, for Stein, allows the experience of being to persist in consciousness, but the very being of the ego itself, as it lives, is an actual being.

It is the being of the ego that introduces for Stein a limit, which brings us to the third aspect of the present. Whereas Perone's present is marked by the limits of finitude, Stein's view of the present made living in an ego admits a finitude that requires it to be constantly held in being: being needs to be given to the finite ego in order for it to live, especially as the ego's life is subject to passing and, therefore, nonbeing. The actual living of the ego from moment to moment in the actuality of the lived experience is only temporary and, therefore, fleeting. The ego can never stop the flow of lived experiences, and as such is never in control of its own being. It receives experiences, and therefore experiences itself as received in experience; and its being is experienced as an *empfangenes Sein,* a received being.[75] The ego does not call itself into being, but finds itself already "thrown into being" (FEB 54). What begins in a very Husserlian fashion with a meditation on the nature of lived experience and what lies behind experience, namely, the pure I, is now elaborated. Stein goes on to analyze the very being of that I through the Heideggerian-inspired notions of time and being. Temporality reveals our being as fleeting and the fact that we are not in full possession of our being.

What, then, is the nature of this received being? Stein begins to speak of this received being as a nihilating being *(nichtiges Sein)* because it is fleeting. Moment to moment this being that I find myself immersed in disappears (FEB 53). Yet, despite this nonbeing, I continue to exist. One finds oneself continuing to be as well as experiencing a fleeting of being. For Stein, however, this being of the *nichtiges Sein* points to a fullness (FEB 53). The fact that being possesses the doubleness of not-being and being concomitant with the fact that there is a continuous flow of this experience of being suggests that being is also a becoming. As one moment disappears, another moment is given. The I is that concrete unity that makes the experience of the moments of being livable, not as mere unconnected moments, but as a whole life unified within the dynamic of the I.

Having accepted Husserl's understanding of the pure I as unifier of experience and Heidegger's insight into the fleeting nature of being as a *nichtiges Sein*, Stein goes on to give her own phenomenological description of the being of the I, namely: the I as being-kept-in-being (... *im Sein erhalten*). Stein experiences the being of the I not only as fleeting, but as constantly reaffirmed because it is kept-in-being. This being-kept-in-being is experienced as peace and security, the sweet, content security of a child. Being is constantly being given to the I. Stein claims Heidegger's notion of *Angst* as a fundamental *Lebensgefühl* [a feeling of life] is given much too much emphasis (FEB 56).

Although *Angst* is a legitimate feeling as we consider our own imminent deaths, it is not the only experience.[76] The experience of our beings constantly being held-in-being and the security that our beings will be definitely held-in-being signify a comfort or certainty in our being—a *Seinssicherheit* (FEB 58). If we accept Stein's analysis, we can posit the possibility that the angst and negative feelings associated with impasse are perhaps not as totalizing as we think they are. She breaks the force or pressure of the condition we find ourselves in by reminding us that our being is not reducible to the impasse and that our being persists otherwise than what the impasse determines or conditions. We are kept in being despite the noxious stagnation of the impasse: being is given, and it does not come from the impasse itself, which seeks to stymie or block being.

The experience of being-kept-in-being and the sweet security that accompanies such an experience of the being of the I causes Stein to question her experience more fully. From whence does my being receive its being? In other words, what or who keeps my being continually becoming until my death, especially given that I experience myself as not being capable of giving myself being? Stein affirms there is an other who preserves my being (FEB 57–58). The being of the I is experienced as "stopping in" and grounded in a being who is groundless and "stopless"—an eternal being. Stein's phenomenology of the I opens up the field of experience to reveal that our beings are preserved in a being that is experienced as endless and groundless. Philosophy and phenomenology stop here, for Stein. They can go no further in naming this experience of being-preserved-in-being by an eternal Being who continually gives our being to us despite the very fleeting of being. This existing despite the fleeting moments of being into nothingness is confirmed in the very experience of the ego to identify itself as "I am" despite the fleeting of my being.

When philosophy and phenomenology reach their human limit, Stein appeals to the knowledge of faith. Faith is not to be conceived as blind consent, for that would result in a fideism of the worst sort. Rather, faith is to be conceived as a kind of knowing, a knowing based on spiritual sensibilities.[77] It is not like rational or intellectual knowing although it draws on these human faculties. Faith is to be understood in the English sense of "belief" wherein one need not have things confirmed each and every time. Stein's notion of faith follows very much the Thomistic and Scholastic line of thought in which faith works within the dynamic of human reason and will. That is, *fides quaerens intellectum* (faith seeking understanding). Faith, then, is not to be conceived as opposed to rationality. It is another way of knowing.

Stein claims there are two ways in which one can describe the experience of the other that holds our beings in being. First, one can turn to Revelation given in Faith. This other, then, becomes identified as the personal God of Scripture and Tradition (FEB 58). The second way is by appealing to thought illumined by faith, a more philosophical approach. One can, like Thomas, try to give proofs for the existence of the Eternal Being, described as First Cause, Pure Being, First Mover, Ultimate Telos, and so on. Through thinking about proofs for the existence of God, one comes to a deeper understanding of the nature of the Being who preserves our being as an "I am," despite the fleeting of our being into moments of nonbeing or nothingness (FEB 58).

Lingering and Security in Being: A Dialectical Relationship?

Perone's and Stein's analyses give us a present in which we can linger, and in which we can feel ourselves being given more being, all in impasse. I see these two ways of being as interrelated in that lingering is made possible by a feeling of ease, comfort, and security: we can linger awhile, we can think when we know there is no future task that requires our attention or when there is a lack of Heideggerian anxiety over the radical finitude (death) of time, as both Perone and Stein, *contra* Heidegger, point out. Lingering and the safe expectation that being will be given imply an opening of a time-space in which one can be in a moment in impasse, a moment that can be experienced in a durational sense. This time-space has to be open, that is, it has to be experienced with both beginning and end receding into a background in order for one to live fully in that present moment. In addition, it must be noted that both lingering and security stand in an important relation to one another. The security in being permits a lingering, but the lingering also reinforces the awareness that being is constantly being given to us in that very lived experience of the present. The lingering in impasse as the threshold of the present can be rendered more intense with the knowledge and/or feeling that this threshold of possibility can persist. The certainty that comes from a security in being, while in the impasse, can, in turn, make the initiative of being a subject and of dilating the present more possible.

Possibility and impossibility are subject to time. They are experienced and lived not only quantitatively, that is, in a measurable time of instants, but in the qualitative sense of a Steinian durational content of becoming, as a lived experience. For example, in a threshold experience, the subject can choose to dilate the present by making present a possibility for its being; but if that possibility of being is simply fleeting, or if it really moves and grasps the subject, this experience reveals a certain intensity to a possibility, an intensity of personal being that Stein has called "depth."[78] The experience of a qualitative experience of possibility can be more or less possible, realizable, or achievable. The possibility can also resonate with one aspect of the subject's being or even with the whole, or with no part of the subject's being at all. For example, a possibility emerges in a threshold experience: the wish to be a writer or poet. This desire can move my entire being: it can be seen as a vocation, understood in the traditional sense as a way of being or even a personal identity. In the same threshold experience, the possibility of writing may emerge in a less intense way, perhaps as a fleeting desire: it would be nice to be a writer, but I know that I do not possess the talents. I consider this possibility for a brief time, in the present, before dismissing it. My dismissal results in a closure of a possibility for the subject arrived in the threshold experience.

What contributes and helps to intensify possibility? What helps possibility seem more achievable, ultimately dilating the possible present maximally, especially in impasse? Stein is right to affirm that the degree of depth of the experience of possibility helps make it seem more real or possible, but I also believe her discussion of security in being and the transcendence it announces can make the experience of possibility more realizable, more possible. The security that derives from the awareness that being is given and will be given from moment to moment can give to the experience of possibility in the threshold or in lived experience of the duration a strong foundation in being that renders the very experience of possibility more solid, more achievable, closer to our being, and more meaningful. The more a possibility is held secure in being, the more it seems realizable and real, and the less it appears as impossible. When possibility emerges within a Heideggerian framework of being-towards-death and anxiety, it will more easily, and perhaps even more intensely, turn to impossibility. What, in the impasse, allows possibility to linger, what allows it to flood the depths of our being, is the fact that it is not erased by anxiety or by the closure of the present moving into a having been of the past. The feeling and knowledge that the possibility can endure in the present gives us hope and confidence that it can be achieved, that it is not impossible. Stein gives to Perone's possibility of dilation the experience of security in being, which can ultimately color the way the dilation happens, with more or less depth, with more or less intensity, and, therefore, with greater or lesser possibility. The depth and the intensity of the lived experience of possibility are directly affected by the way it is lived psychically and existentially. The comfort and ease that comes with a Steinian security in being conditions the very quality of the possibility announced by Perone's threshold experience.

Furthermore, Stein's argument that a security in being points to another kind of being that gives being to us and holds us in it, namely, God, creates in us a knowledge of our own finite limits, which are being held in being by an eternal, infinite being. Stein admits that in the experience of our very being, we expect and indeed hope that our being will persist, that more being will come. We trust that it will; there is hope and confidence. In fact, according to Stein, hope and expectation are built into the very structure of our being, as we anticipate God will not only hold us in being but also preserve us in being. In the impasse, our finitude, in a deep sense, is constantly being given the potential to be and live; in every moment that being is being given, that we are being held in being, we transcend our own finitude. This experience can bend back to color own experience of possibility.

Here, we uncover the deep structure of ultimate hope in the impasse, a hope that things may be possible even though we have come to a limit, the limit of our very own finitude. The radical transcendence announced by Stein in her analysis of the living present gives to the experience of possibility an ultimate possibility, namely, that impossibility may be transcended, may be overcome through God's giving another possibility to us in the form of the givenness of being, a being that we anticipate moment to moment as we rest secure in our being. Possibility, then, need not be framed within the extension of our own finite limits, but can be altered radically by God's making possible that which is impossible for us. Hope, ultimate hope, cannot be understood simply as a possibility within the realms of all possible finite possibilities; it requires a radical break with all that is possible in a given realm. For Stein, our finitude, the very structure of who and what we are as beings, is constantly being given being which finite beings cannot give themselves—namely, life. With every new moment of life comes the possibility of God's giving more possibility to a finite being, possibility that may transcend the limits of our possibility. Stein's analysis of the security in being and the givenness of being by God adds to the threshold experience of the subjective dilation of a maximum possibility, namely, the possibility of overcoming that which may appear impossible, which is the true sense of hope. Hope, the ultimate and maximal form of possibility lies, Stein believes, within the very experience of the durational present. This radical hope of possibility that can transcend the impossible impasse can condition the very possibility announced in Perone's threshold experience of the subject's dilating present, ultimately giving to the subject the possibility of radical transcendence of the impasse from within.

Conclusion: On Possible New Forms of Selfhood

Impasse can be a revelatory moment of political life. Traditionally viewed as stagnation, inaction, and impossibility, there are times when impasse undeniably appears in the aforementioned forms. But the unique moment of history we currently live, in which new scales and structures of global and globalizing social and political orders emerge, has also restructured the very being of impasse, revealing a massive amount of people who find themselves in the neither–nor of political rule, somewhere between the ruler and the ruled. The scale and pressure of such an impasse, with its overwhelming feeling of no outside and the stymying of genuine political possibilities, push inward those who suffer the impasse. This pressure causes the self to feel itself, to live itself in auto-affection, in ways that desire to resist the impasse, at least from within.

The vision and experience of the self, the modern self, understood as autonomous and in control of its internal and external realms, is blocked by impasse. Impasse forces us to renegotiate the way we relate to and value ourselves. And rather than the self of identity, the substantial self of traditional Western philosophy, we discover that we can stand in relation to ourselves in a new way: we can work to be at home with ourselves as we build ourselves in oikeiotic self-fashioning. It is and through this oikeiotic process that we feel ourselves anew, that we see the importance of world building and culture building. Impasse also helps activate, even generating new, inner possibilities of thinking, willing, judging, and imagining, while pushing us to act upon ourselves. It is this remaking of ourselves, finding a new home for ourselves in the hard work of self-recovery, that new political possibilities can be imagined and thought in which new forms of social and political agency can emerge. It is also a process that can fortify the self by reconfiguring one's inner life, ultimately resisting the sometimes negative and violent realities of the external world by creating and abiding in an inner home in which one learns to see oneself, others, and the world in other ways. Part of political life and thinking consists in finding ways to transform how we understand ourselves. As the I of modernity wanes, besieged by the nihilism that Nietzsche so tragically described, perhaps through impasse and its oikeiotic possibilities, we can resist, transform, or even create new forms of power, political life, and subjectivity.

NOTES

Preface

1 See the works of Naomi Klein, in particular *No Logo* (New York: Picador, 2009) and *This Changes Everything: Capitalism vs. the Climate* (New York: Simon and Schuster, 2015).

2 Chantal Mouffe, *For a Left Populism* (London: Verso, 2018), 24–5.

3 Kimberlé Crenshaw, "Demarginalizing the Intersection of Race and Sex: A Black Feminist Critique of Antidiscrimination Doctrine, Feminist Theory and Antiracist Politics", in University of Chicago Legal Forum, no. 1, 1989, 139–67; Chandra Talpade Mohanty, *Feminism without Borders: Decolonizing Theory, Practicing Solidarity* (Durham, NC: Duke University Press, 2003).

4 Peter Fleming, *The Death of Homo Economicus: Work, Debt, and the Myth of Endless Accumulation* (London: Pluto Press, 2017), 130–71.

5 Mouffe, *For a Left Populism*, 33–4.

6 Milton Friedman, "Neo-Liberalism and Its Prospects", in *Faramand*, February 17, 1951, 89–93.

Chapter 1

1 Mouffe, *For a Left Populism*, 32.

2 Rosa Luxemburg, "Reform or Revolution?" in *Reform or Revolution and Other Writings* (New York: Dover Publications, 2006), 3–76.

3 Michel Foucault, "The Subject and Power," in *Critical Inquiry*, vol. 8, no. 4 (Summer 1982), 777–95.

4   Zygmunt Bauman, *Liquid Modernity* (Cambridge, MA: Polity, 2000).

5   Noam Chomsky, *The Prosperous Few and the Restless Many: Interviews with Noam Chomsky* (with David Basmarian) (Bolder, CO: Odonian Press, 1993), 1–12.

6   Christian Marazzi, *The Violence of Financial Capitalism*, trans. Kristina Lebedeva and Jason Francis McGimsey (Los Angeles: Semiotext(e), 2011), 120–1.

7   Ibid., 49.

8   Christian Lotz, *The Capitalist Scheme: Time, Money and the Culture of Abstraction* (Lanham, MD: Lexington Books, 2014).

9   Maurizio Lazzarato, *The Making of the Indebted Man*, trans. Joshua David Jordan (Cambridge, MA: MIT Press, 2012).

10 Elettra Stimilli, *Debt and Guilt: A Political Philosophy* (London: Bloomsbury, 2018). See also her *The Debt of the Living: Ascesis and Capitalism*, trans. Arianna Bove (Albany, NY: State University of New York Press, 2017).

11 Alain Badiou, *Being and Event*, trans. Oliver Feltham (London: Continuum, 2006). French original: *L'Être et l'événement* (Paris: Seuil, 1988). Hereafter parenthetically cited as EE.

12 Franco Berardi, *The Soul at Work: From Alienation to Autonomy* (Los Angeles: Semiotext(e), 2009), 75.

13 Marazzi, *The Violence of Financial Capitalism*, 44–5.

Chapter 2

1   Rei Terada, "Impasse as a Figure of Political Space," in *Comparative Literature*, vol. 72, no. 2 2020, 144–58, 144.

2   Emily Apter, *Unexceptional Politics: On Obstruction, Impasse, and the Impolitic* (London: Verso: 2018), 9, 16, 34. See also Terada, "Impasse as a Figure of Political Space," 157.

3   Ibid.

4   Ibid.

5   Alain Badiou, *Manifesto for Philosophy*, trans. Norman Madarasz (Albany, NY: State University of New York Press, 1999), 79–82.

6   Alain Badiou, *Abrégé de métapolitique* (Paris: Seuil, 1998), 156–60. Hereafter parenthetically cited as AM.

7   Parts of this section on Badiou have been taken and reworked from my earlier work on the French philosopher. See Antonio Calcagno, "Can Alain Badiou's Notion of Time Account for Political Events?" in *International Studies in Philosophy*, vol. 37, no. 2, 2005, 1–14. See also Antonio Calcagno, "Alain Badiou: The Event of Becoming a Political Subject," in Philosophy and Social Criticism, vol. 34, November 2008, 1051–71, and "Alain Badiou's Suturing of the Law to the Event and the State of Exception," in Journal of French and Francophone Philosophy, vol. 24, no. 1, 2016, 192–204, DOI 10/5195/jffp.2016.712.

8   Badiou, *L'Être et l'événement*, 194. Hereafter parenthetically cited as EE.

9   Antonio Calcagno, *Badiou and Derrida: Politics, Events and Their Time* (London: Continuum, 2007).

10 Michael Hardt and Antonio Negri, *Empire* (Cambridge, MA: Harvard University Press, 2001) and Alain Badiou, *D'un désastre obscur: Sur la fin de la vérité d'État* (Paris: Aube, 1999).

11 Michel Foucault, *The History of Sexuality*, vol. 1, trans. Charles Hurley (New York: Pantheon Books, 1978).

12 Ibid., 92.

13 Ibid., 92–3.

14 Ibid., 93.

15 Ibid., 94.

16 Ibid.

17 Ibid.

18 Ibid., 95.

19 Ibid., 95–6.

20 Foucault, "The Subject and Power," 777.

21 Ibid., 777–9.

22 Ibid., 781.

23 Ibid., 788.

24 Ibid., 789.

25 Ibid.

26 Ibid.

27 Ibid., 792.

28 Ibid., 793.

29 Ibid.

30 "For, if it is true that at the heart of power relations and as a permanent condition of their existence there is an insubordination and a certain essential obstinacy on the part of the principles of freedom, then there is no relationship of power without the means of escape or possible flight. Every power relationship implies, at least *in potentia*, a strategy of struggle, in which the two forces are not superimposed, do not lose their specific nature, or do not finally become confused. Each constitutes for the other a kind of permanent limit, a point of possible reversal. A relationship of confrontation reaches its term, its final moment (and the victory of one of the two adversaries), when stable mechanisms replace the free play of antagonistic reactions. Through such mechanisms one can direct, in a fairly constant manner and with reasonable certainty, the conduct of others. For a relationship of confrontation, from the moment it is not a struggle to the death, the fixing of a power relationship becomes a target—at one and the same time its fulfillment and its suspension. And in return, the strategy of struggle also constitutes a frontier for the relationship of power, the line at which, instead of manipulating and inducing actions in a calculated manner, one must be content with reacting to them after the event. It would not be possible for power relations to exist without points of insubordination which, by definition, are means of escape." Ibid., 794.

31 "For, if it is true that at the heart of power relations and as a permanent condition of their existence there is an insubordination and a certain essential obstinacy on the part of the principles of freedom, then there is no relationship of power without the means of escape or possible flight. Every power relationship implies, at least *in potentia*, a strategy of struggle, in which the two forces are not superimposed, do not lose their specific nature, or do not finally become confused. Each constitutes for the other a kind of permanent limit, a point of possible reversal. A relationship of confrontation reaches its term, its final moment (and the victory of one of the two adversaries), when stable mechanisms replace the free play of antagonistic reactions. Through such mechanisms one can direct, in a fairly constant manner and with reasonable certainty, the conduct of others. For a relationship of confrontation, from the moment

it is not a struggle to the death, the fixing of a power relationship becomes a target—at one and the same time its fulfillment and its suspension. And in return, the strategy of struggle also constitutes a frontier for the relationship of power, the line at which, instead of manipulating and inducing actions in a calculated manner, one must be content with reacting to them after the event. It would not be possible for power relations to exist without points of insubordination which, by definition, are means of escape." Ibid., 795.

32 Gilles Deleuze, "Postscript on the Societies of Control," in *October*, vol. 59. (Winter), 1992, 3-7.

33 Ibid., 7.

34 Ibid., 3-4.

35 Ibid., 4.

36 Ibid., 4-5.

37 Ibid., 6.

38 Shoshana Zuboff, *The Age of Surveillance Capitalism: The Fight for a Human Future at the Frontier of Power* (New York: PublicAffairs, 2019).

39 Deleuze, "Postscript...," 7-8.

40 Roberto Esposito, "Outside of Thought," in *Roberto Esposito: New Directions in Biophilosophy* (Edinburgh: Edinburgh University Press, 2021).

41 Part of this section on Esposito draws from an earlier article, Antonio Calcagno, "The Possibility of Resistance in Roberto Esposito's Account of Persons and Things," in *The Concept of Resistance in Italy: Multidisciplinary Perspectives*, eds. Maria Laura Mosco and Pietro Pirani (London: Rowman and Littlefield International, 2017), 193-208. I am grateful to the publisher for the permission to produce parts of it here.

42 Roberto Esposito, *Immunitas: The Protection and Negation of Life*, trans. Zakiya Hanafi (London: Polity Press, 2011). Hereafter parenthetically cited as IM.

43 Roberto Esposito, *Living Thought: The Origins and Actuality of Italian Philosophy*, trans. Zakiya Hanafi (Paolo Alto, CA: Stanford University Press, 2012), 157-70.

44 Roberto Esposito, *Third Person*, trans. Zakiya Hanafi (London: Polity Press, 2012). English translation of: Roberto Esposito, *Terza persona* (Torino: Einaudi, 2007). Hereafter parenthetically cited as TP.

45 Roberto Esposito, *Le persone e le cose* [*Persons and Things*] (Torino: Einaudi, 2014). Hereafter parenthetically cited as PC.

46 "*Il motivo per il quale il corpo eccede la grande divisione tra cose e persone sta nel fatto che non è ascrivibile né alle une né alle altre*" (PC 88).

47 "*Se il diritto tende a cancellare il corpo, la filosofia lo include nel proprio orizzonte—ma nella forma della sua subordinazione. Senza ripetere il gesto escludente della metafisica platonica, ma senza neanche lasciarselo del tutto alle spalle, il pensiero moderno situa il corpo nel registro dell'oggetto. Esso è ciò che il soggetto riconosce, all'interno di se stesso, diverso da sé. Per poterne trattare, egli deve separarsene e tenerlo a distanza. In questo senso la posizione di Cartesio appare esemplare*" (PC 80).

48 "*Naturalmente il ponte mobile che si collega agli oggetti tecnici è il nostro stesso corpo. Non solo la mente, da cui essi traggono le loro caratteristiche funzionali e simboliche, ma anche i segni corporei che sono depositati in essi nell'atto della loro invenzione. Il passaggio di mano in mano, da parte di chi li ha adoperati, crea un flusso continuo che va al di là del singolo individuo per coinvolgere quella dimensione 'transindividuale' alla quale Simondon ha dedicato la propria opera maggiore*" (PC 100).

49 "*Qualcosa, del corpo politico, resta fuori dai suoi confine. Quando ingenti masse si accalcano nelle piazze di mezzo mondo, come oggi sta accadendo, viene allo scoperto qualcosa che precede anche le loro rivendicazioni. Prima ancora di essere pronunciate, le loro parole sono incarnate in corpi che si muovono all'unisono, con il medesimo ritmo, in un'unica onda emotiva. Per quanto possa funzionare come luogo di mobilitazione, senza corpi viventi saldati dalla stessa energia, neanche la rete può essere il nuovo soggetto della politica a venire. Fin da quando fu formulato, nell'evento costituente della prima democrazia moderna, l'enunciato 'noi il popolo' aveva un carattere performativo—produceva l'effetto di creare quanto dichiarava. Da allora ogni atto linguistico che voglia incidere sulla scena politica richiede una bocca e una golla, un respiro di corpi abbastanza vicini da sentire ciò che l'altro dice e da vedere ciò che tutti vedono*" (PC 110).

50 Plato, "Euthyphro," in *Plato: Five Dialogues*, trans. G.M.A. Grube and John M. Cooper (Indianapolis: Hackett, 2002), 1–20.

51 Hannah Arendt, "Thinking," in *The Life of the Mind* (New York: Harcourt, 1971), 172–9.

52 Ibid., 215.

53 Hannah Arendt, "Thinking and Moral Considerations," in *Responsibility and Judgment*, ed. Jerome Kohn (New York: Schocken Books, 2003), 181.

54　Bill Martin, *Politics in the Impasse: Explorations in Post-Secular Theory* (Albany, NY: State University of New York Press, 1996), 172.

55　Donald Kalff, "The EU's Political Impasse: New Economic Opportunities," in *Public Policy Research*, June–August 2006, 96–101, 96.

56　Melissa Rossi, "Moldova's Ongoing Political Impasse," in *The New Presence: Prague's Journal of Central European Philosophy*, Summer 2011, 34–40.

57　Justus Lipsius, *On Constancy*, trans. John Sellars (Liverpool: Liverpool University Press, 2006).

Chapter 3

1　Lazzarato, *The Making of the Indebted Man*.

2　Frank Thieß, "*Die innere Emigration*," Münchner Zeitung, 18 August 1945. Reprinted in Johannes F. G. Grosser, *Die große Kontroverse: Ein Briefwechsel um Deutschland* (Hamburg: Nagel Verlag, 1963), 22–5.

3　See *Flight of Fantasy: New Perspectives on Inner Emigration in German Literature 1933–1945*, eds. Neil H. Donahue and Doris Kirchner (New York: Berghahn Books, 2003).

4　See Michael Philipp, "Distanz und Anpassung: Sozialgeschichtliche Aspekte der Inneren Emigration," in Aspekte der künstlerischen inneren Emigration 1933–1945, Exilforschung Band 12, eds. Claus-Dieter Krohn, Erwin Rotermund, Lutz Winckler and Wulf Koepke (München: edition text + kritik, 1994).

5　"In comparison with the insane end-result—concentration-camp society—the process by which men are prepared for this end, and the methods by which individuals are adapted to these conditions, are transparent and logical. The insane mass manufacture of corpses is preceded by the historically and politically intelligible preparation of living corpses. The impetus and what is more important, the silent consent to such unprecedented conditions are the products of those events which in a period of political disintegration suddenly and unexpectedly made hundreds of thousands of human beings homeless, stateless, outlawed and unwanted, while millions of human beings were made economically superfluous and socially burdensome by unemployment. This in turn could only happen because the Rights of Man, which had never been philosophically established but merely formulated, which had never been politically secured but merely proclaimed, have, in their traditional form, lost all validity." Hannah Arendt, *The Origins of Totalitarianism* (New York: Harcourt Brace, 1979), 447.

6   "The totalitarian attempt at global conquest and total domination has been the destructive way out of all impasses. Its victory may coincide with the destruction of humanity; wherever it has ruled, it has begun to destroy the essence of man. Yet to turn our backs on the destructive forces of the century is of little avail." Ibid., viii.

7   Edith Stein, *Philosophy of Psychology and the Humanities*, trans. Mary Catharine Baseheart and Marianne Sawicki (Washington, DC: ICS Publications, 2000), 7. Hereafter parenthetically cited as PPH.

8   Parts of the following discussion of Michel Henry's philosophy have been taken from my earlier article: "On the Possibility and Impossibility of a World," in *MOSAIC: an interdisciplinary, critical journal*, vol. 51, no. 4, December 2018, 1–9.

9   Michel Henry, *L'essence de la manifestation* (Paris: Presses Universitaires de France, 2003), 59–71; 163–75. Hereafter parenthetically cited as EM.

10 Michel Henry, *L'Incarnation: Une philosophie de la chair* (Paris: Seuil, 2001), 172.

11 Edmund Husserl, *Cartesian Meditations: An Introduction to Phenomenology*, trans. Dorion Cairns (Dordrecht: Springer, 1977).

12 Angela Ales Bello, *The Sense of Things: Toward a Phenomenological Realism*, trans. Antonio Calcagno, in *Analecta Husserliana: The Yearbook of Phenomenological Research* (Dordrecht: Springer, 2015), 58–9.

13 Michel Henry, *La Barbarie* (Paris: Presses Universitaires de Paris, 1987), 14–15; Also EM 289–306.

14 Henry, *L'Incarnation*, 103.

15 Henry, *La Barbarie*, 101–3.

16 Ibid., 15–20.

17 Maurice Merleau-Ponty, *The Visible and the Invisible*, trans. Alphonso Lingis (Evanston, IL: Northwestern University Press, 1968), 135.

18 Henry, *La barbarie*, 201–39.

19 Thomas Langan, *Tradition and Authenticity in the Search for Ecumenic Wisdom* (Columbia, MO: University of Missouri Press, 1992).

20 Parts of this section on Henry and culture are taken and reworked from an earlier article: Antonio Calcagno, "Reclaiming the Possibility of an Interior Human Culture? Michel Henry and *La Barbarie*," in *The Journal of the British Society for Phenomenology*, vol. 44, no. 3, October 2013, 252–65.

21 Henry, *La barbarie*, 4.

22 Ibid., 3 and 165.

23 Michel Henry, *L'auto-donation* (Paris: Édition Prétainte, 2002).

24 Henry, *La barbarie*, 14, 175.

25 G.W.F. Hegel, *The Phenomenology of Spirit*, trans. A.V. Miller (Oxford: Oxford University Press, 1977), 298.

26 Dan Zahavi, "Subjectivity and Immanence in Michel Henry," in *Subjectivity and Transcendence*, ed. A. Grøn, I. Damgaard, and S. Overgaard (Tübingen: Mohr Siebeck, 2007), 133.

27 See Henry's *Incarnation*. See also, Antonio Calcagno, "The Incarnation: Michel Henry and the Possibility of an Husserlian-Inspired Transcendental Life," *The Heythrop Journal*, vol. 45, July 2004, 290–304.

28 Zahavi, "Subjectivity and Immanence," 4–5.

29 Henry, *La barbarie*, 14.

30 Ibid., 4.

31 Henry, *La barbarie*, 15.

32 Ibid., 50–1.

33 Michel Henry, *Voir l'invisible. Sur Kandinsky* (Paris: PUF, 2005).

34 Michel Henry, *Incarnation*, 139–48.

35 Henry, *La barbarie*, 127.

36 Ibid., 71.

37 Ibid., 172.

38 Ibid., 132.

39 Ibid., 36–7.

40 Ibid., 162.

41 Hannah Arendt, *Love and Saint Augustine*, trans. J. Vecchiarelli Scott and J. Chelius Stark (Chicago: University of Chicago Press, 1996), 24.

42 Iris Marion Young, "Responsibility and Global Justice: A Social Connection Model", in *Social Philosophy and Policy*, vol. 23, no. 1, January 2006, 102–30.

43 Pierre Hadot, *The Inner Citadel: The Meditations of Marcus Aurelius*, trans. Michael Chase (Cambridge, MA: Harvard University Press, 2001).

44 Hannah Arendt, *Lectures on Kant's Political Philosophy*, ed. Ronald Beiner (Chicago: University of Chicago Press, 1989).

45 Ibid., 20-2.

46 "*Il fondamento unico della singolarità e dell'universalità della persona è l'iniziativa. Infatti l'iniziativa per un verso concreta e quindi singolarizza la persona, per l'altro la invalora e quindi la universalizza. L'iniziativa è a un tempo esigenza, decisione e valutazione: la decisione offre una determinzaione all'esigenza, e quindi la concreta e la singolarizza; la valutazione pone tale determinazione su un piano di valore, e quindi la invalora e la universalizza.*" Luigi Pareyson, *Esistenza e Persona* (Genova: Il Melangolo, 1985), 168.

47 "*Il fondamento unico della singolarità e dell'universalità della persona è l'iniziativa. Infatti l'iniziativa per un verso concreta e quindi singolarizza la persona, per l'altro la invalora e quindi la universalizza. L'iniziativa è a un tempo esigenza, decisione e valutazione: la decisione offre una determinzaione all'esigenza, e quindi la concreta e la singolarizza; la valutazione pone tale determinazione su un piano di valore, e quindi la invalora e la universalizza.*" Ibid., 169.

48 Citation continues: "Thus criminals, who for other reasons are an essential element in concentration-camp society, are ordinarily sent to a camp only on completion of their prison sentence. Under all circumstances totalitarian domination sees to it that the categories gathered in the camps—Jews, carriers of disease, representatives of dying classes—have already lost their capacity for both normal or criminal action." Arendt, *The Origins of Totalitarianism*, 145.

49 Ibid., 150.

50 Augustine, *Confessions*, trans. Henry Chadwick (Oxford: Oxford University Press, 2009), 299.

51 Edith Stein, "Philosophy of Psychology and the Humanities," in *The Collected Works of Edition Stein*, vol. 7 (Washington, DC: ICS Publications, 2000), Kindle Edition, 41.

52 Ibid.

53 Ibid., 42.

54 Edith Stein, "*Der Aufbau der menschlichen Person*," ed. Beate Beckmann-Zöller, in *Edith Stein Gesamtausgabe* (Freiburg-im-Breisgau, Germany: Herder, 2004), 123.

55 See Joseph Torchia, O.P., *Restless Mind: "Curiositas" and the Scope of Inquiry in St. Augustine's Psychology* (Milwaukee: Marquette University Press, 2013).

56 Henry, *L'essence de la manifestation*.

57 Stein, *Philosophy of Psychology and the Humanities*, 133.

58 Ibid., 134.

59 Ibid.

60 Ibid.

61 Ibid., 136–7.

62 Ibid., 137.

63 Ibid.

64 Gerda Walther, *Phänomenologie der Mystik* (Freiburg im B.: Walter Verlag, 1955), 39.

65 Parts of this section on time are taken and reworked from a previously published chapter, "Lingering Gifts of Time: Ugo Perone, Edith Stein and Martin Heidegger's Philosophical Legacy," in *Open Borders: Encounters between Italian Philosophy and Continental Thought*, eds. Silvia Benso and Antonio Calcagno (Albany, NY: State University of New York Press, 2022).

66 Ugo Perone, *The Possible Present*, trans. Silvia Benso with Brian Schroeder (Albany, NY: State University of New York Press, 2012). Hereafter parenthetically cited as PP.

67 Edith Stein, *Finite and Eternal Being*, trans. K. Reinhardt (Washington, DC: ICS Publications, 2002). Hereafter parenthetically cited as FEB.

68 Perone remarks, "[The present] cannot be a simple limit, that is, [it cannot be] the extreme line either of a contact defining itself through separation or

of a being whose consistency is given through exclusion or of an encounter stiffening differences. Nor is it properly a barrier, because the barrier is simultaneously insurmountable and independent from me. The divide is instead mobile, and a constructive trait of the deciding subject. Nor is [the divide] of the absolute that tangentially encounters the infinite, the *eschaton* that becomes time, because the divide does not discriminate absolutely but rather chooses on the basis of finitude, reorients finitude, and arranges it within the order of time" (PP 16).

69 Pareyson, *Esistenza e persona*, 168.

70 See Enrico Guglielminetti, *Interruzioni. Note sulla filosofia di Ugo Perone* (Genoa: Il Nuovo Melangolo, 2006), 18.

71 Ugo Perone, *Nonostante il soggetto* (Turin: Rosenberg and Sellier, 1995). See also Ugo Perone, *La verità del sentimento* (Naples: Guida, 2008) and Ugo Perone, *Ripensare il sentimento. Elementi per una teoria* (Assisi: Cittadella Editrice, 2014).

72 Perone observes, "The present, however, cannot be deferred, that is put off to a new role. Perhaps it can be prolonged through lingering, which expands [it] and gains new time. Lingering remains within the present and prolongs it. Conversely, deferrals feed on indifference. Because all things are the same, times too are the same, and everything slides away and is deferred. The present is instead here, it impends, and it demands a subject that handles it. The time centred on the present is not cosmological but rather human time, which presupposes a subject (not a master) of time. This subject that ventures through time is no longer the solipsistic subject. Having risked itself in existence, having trusted itself to temporality, the subject has encountered the extension of the self. Yet this extension that, as the figure of the threshold has shown to us, always occurs within an alternative between oppositions (outside/inside, past/future) unfolds but not like an inertial expansion. It knows oppositions, fatigue, and rough rubbing, in principle (without wishing to account properly for this here), the subject from now on inevitably finds itself confronted with its own and other's alterity; thus it is open to a possible intersubjectivity first of all because it is indeed implicated in a tangle of intersubjectivity"(PP 27).

73 Ugo Perone, "The Risks of the Present: Benjamin, Bonhoeffer, Celan," *Symposium: Canadian Review of Continental Philosophy*, vol. 14, no. 2 2010, 19–34, 33.

74 Hedwig Conrad Martius, "*Die Zeit*," in *Philosophischer Anzeiger*, vol. 2 and 4, 1927/28, 143–82, 345–90.

75 Received being lies in opposition to Heidegger's *Geworfenessein*.

76 See Sarah Borden Sharkey, *Thine Ownself: Individuality in Edith Stein's Later Writings* (Washington, DC: ICS Publications, 2009); Ken Casey, "Do We Die Alone? Edith Stein's Critique of Heidegger," in *Intersubjectivity, Humanity, Being: Edith Stein's Phenomenology and Christian Philosophy*, eds. Mette Lebech and John Haydn Gurmin (New York: Peter Lang, 2015), 334–8; Vincent Wargo, "Reading against the Grain: Edith Stein's Confrontation with Heidegger as an Encounter with Hermeneutical Ontology," *Journal of the British Society for Phenomenology*, vol. 42, no. 2 2011, 125–38.

77 See Edith Stein, *Ways to Know God*, trans. R. Allers (New York: Edith Stein Guild, 1981), 37–51.

78 Edith Stein, *Der Aufbau der menschlichen Person*, in *Edith Steins Werke*, eds. Lucy Gelber and Michael Linssen (Freiburg: Herder, 1994), vol. 16, 114.

BIBLIOGRAPHY

Ales Bello, Angela, "*The Sense of Things: Toward a Phenomenological Realism*," trans. Antonio Calcagno, in *Analecta Husserliana: The Yearbook of Phenomenological Research* (Dordrecht: Springer, 2015).

Apter, Emily, *Unexceptional Politics: On Obstruction, Impasse, and the Impolitic* (London: Verso, 2018).

Arendt, Hannah, "Thinking," in *The Life of the Mind* (New York: Harcourt, 1971).

Arendt, Hannah, *The Origins of Totalitarianism* (New York: Harcourt Brace, 1979).

Arendt, Hannah, *Lectures on Kant's Political Philosophy*, ed. Ronald Beiner (Chicago: University of Chicago Press, 1989).

Arendt, Hannah, *Love and Saint Augustine*, trans. J. Vecchiarelli Scott and J. Chelius Stark (Chicago: University of Chicago Press, 1996).

Arendt, Hannah, "Thinking and Moral Considerations," in *Responsibility and Judgment*, ed. Jerome Kohn (New York: Schocken Books, 2003), 159–89.

Augustine, *Confessions*, trans. Henry Chadwick (Oxford: Oxford University Press, 2009).

Badiou, Alain, *Being and Event*, trans. Oliver Feltham (London: Continuum, 2006). French original: *L'Être et l'événement* (Paris: Seuil, 1988).

Badiou, Alain, *Abrégé de métapolitique* (Paris: Seuil, 1998).

Badiou, Alain, *D'un désastre obscur: Sur la fin de la vérité d'État* (Paris: Aube, 1999).

Badiou, Alain, *Manifesto for Philosophy*, trans. Norman Madarasz (Albany, NY: State University of New York Press, 1999).

Bauman, Zygmunt, *Liquid Modernity* (Cambridge, MA: Polity, 2000).

Berardi, Franco, *The Soul at Work: From Alienation to Autonomy* (Los Angeles: Semiotext(e), 2009).

Borden Sharkey, Sarah, *Thine Ownself: Individuality in Edith Stein's Later Writings* (Washington, DC: ICS Publications, 2009).

Calcagno, Antonio, "Can Alain Badiou's Notion of Time Account for Political Events?" in *International Studies in Philosophy* 37, 2 (2005): 1–14.

Calcagno, Antonio, *Badiou and Derrida: Politics, Events and Their Time* (London: Continuum, 2007).

Calcagno, Antonio, "Alain Badiou: The Event of Becoming a Political Subject" in *Philosophy and Social Criticism* 34, (November 2008): 1051–71.

Calcagno, Antonio, "Reclaiming the Possibility of an Interior Human Culture? Michel Henry and *La Barbarie*," in *The Journal of the British Society for Phenomenology* 44, 3 (October 2013): 252-65.

Calcagno, Antonio, "Alain Badiou's Suturing of the Law to the Event and the State of Exception," in *Journal of French and Francophone Philosophy* 24, 1 (2016): 192-204.

Calcagno, Antonio, "The Possibility of Resistance in Roberto Esposito's Account of Persons and Things," in *The Concept of Resistance in Italy: Multidisciplinary Perspectives*, eds. Maria Laura Mosco and Pietro Pirani (London: Rowman and Littlefield International, 2017).

Calcagno, Antonio, "On the Possibility and Impossibility of a World," in *MOSAIC: An Interdisciplinary, Critical Journal* 51, 4 (December 2018): 1-9.

Calcagno, Antonio, "Lingering Gifts of Time: Ugo Perone, Edith Stein and Martin Heidegger's Philosophical Legacy," in *Open Borders: Encounters between Italian Philosophy and Continental Thought*, eds. Silvia Benso and Antonio Calcagno (Albany, NY: State University of New York Press, 2021), 113-32.

Casey, Ken, "Do We Die Alone? Edith Stein's Critique of Heidegger," in *Intersubjectivity, Humanity, Being: Edith Stein's Phenomenology and Christian Philosophy*, eds. Mette Lebech and John Haydn Gurmin (New York: Peter Lang, 2015), 334-8.

Chomsky, Noam, *The Prosperous Few and the Restless Many: Interviews with Noam Chomsky* (with David Basmarian) (Boulder, CO: Odonian Press, 1993), 1-12.

Conrad Martius, Hedwig, "Die Zeit," in *Philosophischer Anzeiger* 2 and 4 (1927/28): 143-82, 345-90.

Crenshaw, Kimberlé, "Demarginalizing the Intersection of Race and Sex: A Black Feminist Critique of Antidiscrimination Doctrine, Feminist Theory and Antiracist Politics," in *University of Chicago Legal Forum*, 1 (1989): 139-67.

Donahue, Neil H. and Kirchner, Doris (eds.), *Flight of Fantasy: New Perspectives on Inner Emigration in German Literature 1933-1945* (New York: Berghahn Books, 2003).

Esposito, Roberto, *Immunitas: The Protection and Negation of Life*, trans. Zakiya Hanafi (London: Polity Press, 2011).

Esposito, Roberto, *Living Thought: The Origins and Actuality of Italian Philosophy*, trans. Zakiya Hanafi (Paolo Alto, CA: Stanford University Press, 2012).

Esposito, Roberto, *Third Person*, trans. Zakiya Hanafi (London: Polity Press, 2012). English translation of: Roberto Esposito, *Terza persona* (Torino: Einaudi, 2007).

Esposito, Roberto, *Le persone e le cose* (Torino: Einaudi, 2014).
Fleming, Peter, *The Death of Homo Economicus: Work, Debt, and the Myth of Endless Accumulation* (London: Pluto Press, 2017).
Foucault, Michel, *The History of Sexuality*, vol. 1, trans. Charles Hurley (New York: Pantheon Books, 1978).
Foucault, Michel, "The Subject and Power," in *Critical Inquiry* 8, 4 (Summer 1982): 777–95.
Friedman, Milton, "Neo-Liberalism and Its Prospects," in *Faramand* (February 17, 1951): 89–93.
Guglielminetti, Enrico, *Interruzioni. Note sulla filosofia di Ugo Perone* (Genoa: Il Nuovo Melangolo, 2006).
Hadot, Pierre, *The Inner Citadel: The Meditations of Marcus Aurelius*, trans. Michael Chase (Cambridge, MA: Harvard University Press, 2001).
Hardt, Michael and Negri, Antonio, *Empire* (Cambridge, MA: Harvard University Press, 2001).
Hegel, G.W.F., *The Phenomenology of Spirit*, trans. A.V. Miller (Oxford: Oxford University Press, 1977).
Henry, Michel, *La Barbarie* (Paris: Presses Universitaires de Paris, 1987).
Henry, Michel, *L'Incarnation: Une philosophie de la chair* (Paris: Seuil, 2001).
Henry, Michel, *L'auto-donation* (Paris: Édition Prétainte, 2002).
Henry, Michel, *L'essence de la manifestation* (Paris: Presses Universitaires de France, 2003).
Henry, Michel, *Voir l'invisible. Sur Kandinsky* (Paris: Presses Universitaires de France 2005).
Husserl, Edmund, *Cartesian Meditations: An Introduction to Phenomenology*, trans. Dorion Cairns (Dordrecht: Springer, 1977).
Kalff, Donald, "The EU's Political Impasse: New Economic Opportunities," in *Public Policy Research* (June–August 2006): 96–101.
Klein, Naomi, *No Logo* (New York: Picador, 2009).
Klein, Naomi, *This Changes Everything: Capitalism vs. the Climate* (New York: Simon and Schuster, 2015).
Langan, Thomas, *Tradition and Authenticity in the Search for Ecumenic Wisdom* (Columbia, MO: University of Missouri Press, 1992).
Lazzarato, Maurizio, *The Making of the Indebted Man*, trans. Joshua David Jordan (Cambridge, MA: MIT Press, 2012).
Lipsius, Justus, *On Constancy*, trans. John Sellars (Liverpool: Liverpool University Press, 2006).
Lotz, Christian, *The Capitalist Scheme: Time, Money and the Culture of Abstraction* (Lanham, MD: Lexington Books, 2014).
Luxemburg, Rosa, "Reform or Revolution?" in *Reform or Revolution and Other Writings* (New York: Dover Publications, 2006).

Marazzi, Christian, *The Violence of Financial Capitalism*, trans. Kristina Lebedeva and Jason Mcgimsey, Francis (Los Angeles: Semiotext(e), 2011).
Martin, Bill, *Politics in the Impasse: Explorations in Post-Secular Theory* (Albany, NY: State University of New York Press, 1996).
Merleau-Ponty, Maurice, *The Visible and the Invisible*, trans. Alphonso Lingis (Evanston, IL: Northwestern University Press, 1968).
Mohanty, Chandra Talpade, *Feminism without Borders: Decolonizing Theory, Practicing Solidarity* (Durham, NC: Duke University Press, 2003).
Mouffe, Chantal, *For a Left Populism* (London: Verso, 2018).
Pareyson, Luigi, *Esistenza e persona* (Genova: Il Melangolo, 1985).
Perone, Ugo, *Nonostante il soggetto* (Turin: Rosenberg and Sellier, 1995).
Perone, Ugo, *La verità del sentimento* (Naples: Guida, 2008)
Perone, Ugo, "The Risks of the Present: Benjamin, Bonhoeffer, Celan," *Symposium: Canadian Review of Continental Philosophy* 14, 2 (2010): 19–34, 33.
Perone, Ugo, *The Possible Present*, trans. Silvia Benso with Brian Schroeder (Albany, NY: State University of New York Press, 2012).
Perone, Ugo, *Ripensare il sentimento. Elementi per una teoria* (Assisi: Cittadella Editrice, 2014).
Philipp, Michael, "*Distanz und Anpassung: Sozialgeschichtliche Aspekte der Inneren Emigration*," in *Aspekte der künstlerischen inneren Emigration 1933–1945*, Exilforschung Band 12, eds. Claus-Dieter Krohn, Erwin Rotermund, Lutz Winckler and Wulf Koepke (München: edition text + kritik, 1994).
Plato, "Euthyphro," in *Plato: Five Dialogues*, trans. G.M.A. Grube and John M. Cooper (Indianapolis: Hackett, 2002), 1–20.
Rossi, Melissa, "Moldova's Ongoing Political Impasse," in *The New Presence: Prague's Journal of Central European Philosophy* (Summer 2011): 34–40.
Stein, Edith, *Ways to Know God*, trans. R. Allers (New York: Edith Stein Guild, 1981).
Stein, Edith, *Philosophy of Psychology and the Humanities*, trans. Mary Catharine Bascheart and Marianne Sawicki (Washington, DC: ICS Publications, 2000).
Stein, Edith, *Finite and Eternal Being*, trans. K. Reinhardt (Washington, DC: ICS Publications, 2002).
Stein, Edith, "*Der Aufbau der menschlichen Person*," in *Edith Stein Gesamtausgabe*, ed. Beate Beckmann-Zöller (Freiburg-im-Breisgau: Herder, 2004).
Stimilli, Elettra, *The Debt of the Living: Ascesis and Capitalism*, trans. Arianna Bove (Albany, NY: State University of New York Press, 2017).
Stimilli, Elettra, *Debt and Guilt: A Political Philosophy* (London: Bloomsbury, 2018).
Terada, Rei, "Impasse as a Figure of Political Space," in *Comparative Literature* 72, 2 (2020): 144–58.
Thieß, Frank, "*Die innere Emigration*," Münchner Zeitung, 18, August 1945. Reprinted in Johannes F. G. Grosser, *Die große Kontroverse: Ein Briefwechsel um Deutschland* (Hamburg: Nagel Verlag, 1963), 22–5.

Torchia, Joseph, *Restless Mind: "Curiositas" and the Scope of Inquiry in St. Augustine's Psychology* (Milwaukee: Marquette University Press, 2013).

Walther, Gerda, *Phänomenologie der Mystik* (Freiburg im B: Walter Verlag, 1955), 39.

Wargo, Vincent, "Reading against the Grain: Edith Stein's Confrontation with Heidegger as an Encounter with Hermeneutical Ontology," *Journal of the British Society for Phenomenology* 42, 2 (2011): 125–38.

Young, Iris Marion, "Responsibility and Global Justice: A Social Connection Model," in *Social Philosophy and Policy* 23, 1 (January 2006): 102–30.

Zahavi Dan, "Subjectivity and Immanence in Michel Henry," in *Subjectivity and Transcendence*, eds. A. Grøn, I. Damgaard, and S. Overgaard (Tübingen: Mohr Siebeck, 2007).

INDEX

affective experience
   fundamental capacity 92
   manifestation 84–94
   suffering, example 91
Afghanistan war 1
Ancients, The 65, 73–5, 114, 119
Anders, G., use of new technology 42
annihilation 59–60, 93
   of human species 62
Aquinas, T. 76, 159
Arendt, H. 18, 134
   capitalist consumer societies 3
   on genuine thinking 18
   Human Condition, The 142
   interesse or the being-between 143
   Lectures on Kant's Political Philosophy 126
   Life of the Mind, The 127, 134, 139
   Origins of Totalitarianism 84, 130–1
   on resistance 131
   totalitarianism 3, 131
   view of politics 80
Aristotle 48, 60, 135, 159
   Nicomachean Ethics 75
   philia—neighborly or brotherly love 75–6
   Politics 110
   zoon politikon concept 63
Augustine 110, 134, 140
   Confessions 135
   libido dominandi 77
Aurelius, M. 113
auto-affection 83–6, 88, 90–2, 173
   inner life 94–107

baby boomers 14
   "Cadillac socialists" 15
Badiou, A. 10–11, 34
   possibility and impossibility of impasse 22–8
being
   experience of possibility 168–72
   security in 168–9
   threshold experience 169–70
   two ways of 168
being to nonbeing
   dual perspectives 158–9
   inner experience of time 162
   past and future relationships 159
Bello, A. A. 87
Benjamin, W. 133, 155
Bergson, H.-L. 62, 93, 147, 151
   Creative Evolution 50
   flow of becoming 161–2
bio-capitalism 8
bio-economy 8
biological life
   complete control of 62
   immunological view 61

Canada
   education system 82–3
   impassed living 78–9
   marginal people 80
China, modern changes 11
Chomsky, N. 7
Cicero 74
civil society 11
clonal selection theory 54
Copernicus 133

Dante, defense of rule 4
Deleuze, G. 22, 53, 109
  on immanence of live 49–50
  impasse of the societies of control 40–8
  "Postscript on the Societies of Control" 40
  on resistance 44–5
  A Thousand Plateaus 46–7
Derrida, J. 133
Descartes 56, 158
digital technologies 12–13, 15–16
du Vair, G., notion of political impasse 69
Duvalier (Haiti) 15

Ehrlich, P. 54
Ellul, J., *The Technological Society* 110
Epictetus 74
Epicurus 135
Esposito, R. 109
  on biological life *versus* political life 48, 59–62
  biopolitical regimes 55, 58, 63
  body politics 55–8
  conception of life 58
  on corporeal individuation 51–2
  on Deleuze's idea of becoming 47
  on forms of governmentalization 55
  immunological paradigm 47–53, 55–6, 59, 62–3
  Le persone e le cose 55
  logic of negation 54–5
  on order, conflict, resistance 48–50
  Third Person 49
  view of selfhood 53–5

financial capitalism 12, 14
  crisis development 17
  higher order production 40–1
  new business system 80
  political promise 79
  self-conscious logic 14
  semiocapitalist network 12, 14, 16
First World War 143
Foucault, M. 6, 109
  analyses of power 5, 31, 41
  biopolitical thought 48–9
  History of Sexuality, The 38
  on hope 40
  overcoming of a temporary impasse 28–40
  on resistance 33–5, 39–40
  "The Subject and Power" 34–5
  subjectivation, analysis of 34–5, 38
freedom
  forms of 147–8
  inner experience 148
French Revolution 10
Freud, S. 106

G-7 meetings 35
Galileo 104–5
General Agreement on Trade and Tariffs 16
German Revolution of 1919 2
Germany 70
  Third Reich 83
globalization 20
  international financial market 6–8
  new political order 6, 16
  supply chains 7
governmentality 48, 59, 93
  limits of 62
Gramsci 21, 31
  concept of impasse 19–20

Hadot, P. 113
Hegel, G. W. F.

concept of impasse 19, 21
   master–slave dialectic 73, 76
   Phenomenology of Spirit 90, 97
Heidegger, M. 53, 148, 151, 156
   Being and Time 149
   being-there (*Da-sein*) 74
   on finitude of Dasein 151–2
   fleeting nature of being 165
   on genuine thinking 18
   notion of *Angst* 165
   notions of time and being 165
   presencing of the present 159
Henry, M.
   on human affectivity 102
   La barbarie 94
   life's manifestation 100–3, 106
   logic of *noesis* and *noema* 85–6, 99
   ontological monism 101
   passive view of manifestation 89–90
   passivity and *Empfindungen* 100
   philosophy of culture 95–6, 99–100
   sense experience, examples 87–91
   stages of self-awareness 99
Herodotus 98
Hobbes, T. 3–5
hope
   and confidence 170
   of freedom 147–8
   inner lives 142
   possibilities 50, 84, 132, 141–3, 172
   of resistance 48, 58–64
Husserl 151, 158
   Eigenheitssphäre 80
   Empfindungen 96
   Ich kann or "I can" 97, 137
   insistence on intentionality 86
   nature of lived experience 164–5
   on pure I 165
   sense as the pure ego 163

Idle No More 9
imagination
   constructive ways 119
   contemporary sense of 120
   genuine experience 122
   passive aspects 119
   phantasmata 119
   possibilities during impasse 119–24
   power of 116, 120
   thinking and 65, 118, 120
impasse
   actions of will 129
   breakthrough dynamics 21
   differentiation and repetition processes 46–7
   geopolitical configurations 18
   interior possibilities 121
   inward turn 130–41
   life and death, conflict between 51
   lived experience of time 148–50
   oikeiotic possibility 84
   Platonic urgency 71–2
   reality principle 19–21
International Monetary Fund (IMF) 7, 9, 16

Jankélévitch, V. 113
judgment
   force of 128
   fundamental ways 124
   imagination and 116
   logical operations 68
   possibilities 119
   power of 125–7, 140
   self-becoming *versus* 126

Kalff, D. 69
Kant, I. 114, 124
   notion of judgment 126

Kierkegaard, S. 53
King Jr., M. L. 11
Korean war 1

Langan, T. 95
Lazzarato, M. 8
  indebted man 79
Leibniz, G. W. 62
LGBTQ community 14
Liberal democracy 13, 58
  evolution and devolution
    perspectives 61
Lipsius, J.
  On Constancy 69
  notion of political impasse 69–70
  Stoic philosophy and Christian
    theology 70–1
Louis XIV 11
Louis XVI 11
love or desire
  erotic force 141
  fundamental affects 135
Lucretius, *Dererum natura* 74
Luxemburg, R. 21
  Reform or Revolution? 2

Machiavelli 4–5, 63
  The Prince 40
Marsilius of Padova 4, 133
Martin, B., *Politics in the Impasse:*
  Explorations in Post-Secular
  Theory 69
Martius, H. C., *Die Zeit* 160
Marx, K. 10–12, 15, 30
  Grundrisse 12
May '68 Revolution 10
Merleau-Ponty 137
  Visible and the Invisible 91
Milk, H. 11
monarchic rule 4, 6, 10–11
Mouffe, C. 2

Negri, A. 7, 58
neoliberalism
  economic collapse 2008 2
  financial capitalism 9
  social and political effects 41
Neo-Platonists 4
new impasse. *See also* **Oikeiosis**
  information and computer
    technology, role in 41
  power relation 64–72
NGOs 14
Nicholas of Oresmes 133
Nietzsche 53, 114
  Trotzmacht 112
1960s' civil rights changes 15

Occupy Wall Street 9
Oikeiosis. See also self and selfhood
  auto-affection 83–4
  of inner world 83–4
  Lucretius's idea 74
  modern Western philosophy
    versus 75
  natural process 81, 95
  pressure of impasse 21
  traditional understanding 81–2
Orban, V. (Hungary) 7

Pareyson, L. 128–9, 155
Perone, U. 148, 152–3, 155–8, 160–2
  durational present 158, 163, 168,
    170, 172
  fleeting of being 160
  The Possible Present 149–50
Plato
  conversion of thought 10
  crisis of the Thirty Tyrants 3
  Republic 3, 110
political change
  different forms 6
  historical conditions 1–2, 10

resistance and 6, 48
revolutionary and reformist
  models 15
theoretical models 22
political impasse
  achieved *status quo* 78, 123
  affective thinking 117–20
  affectivity of 95
  apoliteia 111–12, 117
  freedom experience 147–8
  powerful people's self-interest 108
  self-becoming 107–13
  sense of futility 76–7
political power
  forms of anarchism 60
  hierarchy 3–4
political theory 3, 47–8, 60
political thinking 3, 10
populism, forms of 2
power
  central force 31
  conceptions 31–3
  exercise of 36
  five traits 37
  Foucault's definition 36
  logic of 21
  logics and tactics 32–4
  modal structure 37
  resistance, concept of 39–40
  resistance of dominance 64–5
  strategies of 38–9
  traditional concepts 6
  visible and invisible relations 5
present as the threshold 150–8
  Husserlian phenomenology 157
  not-having of time 154–5

real economy 17
resistance
  active thinking 117
  biological life 58–62

concept 39–40
inner turn 84
liberation and 22
personal and impersonal 50–8
political change and 6, 48
political hope 61
power dominance 64–5
temporary impasse 29
Roman model, republican rule 5
ruler–ruled relationship
  classes and 4
  classic division 80
  enforcement of political power
    77–8
  in governmentalized setting 48
  katechonic strategy 21
  subjectivity and selfhood 73–4
Russian Revolution 10

Sartre, J.-P., *Nausea* 123
Second World War 45, 49
self and selfhood 53
  affect of suffering 89, 91
  auto-affection 85–6
  Foucaultian view 64–5
  hope of possibility 147
  horror autotoxicus concept 54
  immunological paradigm 54–5
  katechonizing logic 14
  Lipsius' view 71
  manifestation 101
  memories and experiences 115
  modern I or ego 74
  negative 52–3, 62
  new forms 173–4
  oikeiotic recovery 21
  omnipresence of power 31, 34,
    37
  organizing realm 30
  reflexive experience 107–13
  repository of 117–18

and time 149
society of control
  new forms 43–4
  surveillance capitalism 45
  techno-capitalism 45
Socrates 99, 139
  Phaedrus 139
  Symposium 139
sovereign rule 4–5, 7, 41
Stein, E. 85, 149, 158
  on being and not being 158–60, 168–72
  being of the *nichtiges* 165
  durational present 163
  ego-subject 163–4
  Eigenheitssphäre 80
  Finite and Eternal Being 149, 158
  Gemeinschaftserlebnis, or "lived experience of community 143, 146
  on God 159
  motivation discussion 136–9
  Munster lectures 140
  Philosophy of Psychology 87
  self of collected reflections 114–15
Steinem, G. 11

Terada, concept of impasse 19–20
thinking. *See also* hope; judgment
  deduction and inference 114
  effects of the conversation 113–16
  genuine experience 122
  and imagination 65, 118, 120
  powers of 118
Thucydides 98
Trump, D. 44
2008 crisis 2, 9, 13

Vietnam war 1
Virilio, P., free-floating control 42

wealth creation, debt model 79
Weil, S. 50
Western governments
  immunological paradigm 61
  Liberal economies 10–11
  political crisis, response to 18
  rules, modern forms 5
willing 112, 130, 134–6, 139, 174
  phenomenon of 127–8
world. *See also* auto-affection
  lived present 150
  manifestation from within 84–94

Yellow Jackets movement 35

CPSIA information can be obtained
at www.ICGtesting.com
Printed in the USA
LVHW052003100223
739200LV00007B/754